CONTENTS

ABOVE: Beach reconnaissance teams can be landed covertly from nuclear powered attack submarine. (MOD/CROWN COPYRIGHT)

MAIN COVER IMAGE: (US MARINE CORPS/STAFF SERGEANT KEVIN G. RIVAS)

ISBN: 9781802829334

Editor: Tim Ripley

Data and photo research: Fergus Ripley

Senior editor, specials: Roger Mortimer

Email: roger.mortimer@ keypublishing.com

Cover Design: Steve Donovan

Design: SJmagic DESIGN SERVICES, India

Advertising Sales Manager: Brodie Baxter

Email: brodie.baxter@ keypublishing.com

Tel: 01780 755131

Advertising Production: Becky Antoniades

Email: Rebecca.antoniades@ keypublishing.com

SUBSCRIPTION/MAIL ORDER

Key Publishing Ltd, PO Box 300, Stamford, Lincs, PE9 1NA

Tel: 01780 480404

Subscriptions email: subs@keypublishing.com

Mail Order email: orders@keypublishing.com

Website: www.keypublishing.com/shop

PUBLISHING

Group CEO and Publisher: Adrian Cox

Published by

Key Publishing Ltd, PO Box 100, Stamford, Lincs, PE9 1XQ

Tel: 01780 755131

Website: www.keypublishing.com

PRINTING

Precision Colour Printing Ltd, Haldane, Halesfield 1, Telford, Shropshire. TF7 4QQ

DISTRIBUTION

Seymour Distribution Ltd, 2 Poultry Avenue, London, EC1A 9PU

Enquiries Line: 02074 294000.

BELOW: Amphibious warriors need to be equally at home on the sea as on land. (MOD/CROWN COPYRIGHT)

Beach Assault

Amphibious Warfare in the 21st century

ABOVE: Raising the Stars and Stripes over Iwo Jima February in 1945. It became the iconic image of the US Marine Corps of World War Two in the Pacific. The corps memorial in Washington DC recreated the scene. (DBKING)

Mastering the unpredictable elements of amphibious warfare – tides, soft sand on beaches, and wild weather – are still intrinsic to projecting land forces ashore. Modern marines get just as sea sick in landing craft as Vikings did when they raided the coasts of Europe 1,200 years ago in their long ships.

In *Beach Assault* we aim to review the status of today's amphibious forces around the world. We will examine the tactics of modern amphibious warfare, looking at beach reconnaissance, raiding, beach assault operations and helicopter insertion, as well as explaining the role of amphibious forces in non-combatant evacuations and humanitarian operations.

The status of the world's main amphibious forces will then be reviewed, looking at their units, organisation, and tactics. A key part of a navy's amphibious capability is its specialist shipping to deliver its marines from ship to shore. So, we look at the main types of amphibious ships available around the world.

In this league table of amphibious power, the United States Marine

Projecting military power ashore from the sea is an age-old military art. The Greeks, Romans, and Vikings all built huge empires on the back of being able to land armies on enemy coasts.

Although modern armed forces have more advanced technology, weapons, and ships at their disposal, many of the skills and techniques used in amphibious warfare have their roots back in the ancient era.

RIGHT: On the beach. British Royal Marines during a NATO amphibious exercise in Estonia. (MOD/CROWN COPYRIGHT)

Corps is the undoubted top player with more than 180,000 personnel in its ranks. This makes it bigger than many armies. However, more than 100 countries have dedicated marine or amphibious units, and we aim to look at some of the key amphibious warfare players. We don't have to the space to cover every marine unit in the world, but we hope we capture some of the most interesting, in terms of their organisation, tactics and recent operations.

While modern amphibious operations are the focus of *Beach Assault,* we also look back at some of the most famous amphibious operations over past century. These tell the story of how modern amphibious forces, tactics and technology have developed. The disastrous British and Allied landings at Gallipoli in World War One proved a massive wake-up call and led many armed forces to look seriously to incorporating modern technology to amphibious warfare.

Allied amphibious warfare endeavours in World War Two got off to slow start after Canadian troops suffered heavy losses at Dieppe in 1942. The US and British then built up huge amphibious forces to fight the island-hopping campaign against the Japanese in the Pacific and spearhead the D-Day landings in France.

The techniques, tactics and equipment that helped win World War Two have since been developed by the incorporation of new technology. Modern amphibious forces rely heavily on helicopters to move personnel and equipment ashore, as well as having highly specialised shipping available as launching pads.

The pace of technological development is moving rapidly, and amphibious forces are benefiting from the introduction of water-borne and flying drones, as well as other robotic systems.

We hope you find *Beach Assault* informative and that it helps you understand the unique challenges of amphibious warfare.

Tim Ripley
January 2024

ABOVE: Royal Netherland Marine Corps raiders come ashore in Norway during a NATO exercise to reinforce the alliance's northern flank. (NETHERLANDS MOD)

BELOW: Along with many other countries in the Pacific region, South Korea is building up its amphibious capability. The ROKS *Dokdo* is the pride of the South Korean navy. (US DOD)

ABOVE: Modern amphibious ships are complex machines that are optimised to efficiently deliver fighting forces ashore. (US NAVY)

What is Amphibious Warfare?

Amphibious Tactics and Equipment

The term amphibious warfare conjures up images of massed formations of landing craft approaching the Normandy coast, as German machine gun nests open fire. While the Hollywood movie, *Saving Private Ryan*, brilliantly caught much of the spirit and human experience of amphibious warriors, it gave little insight into the complexity of amphibious warfare.

The essentials of amphibious warfare have not changed since ancient times. It is all about projecting land forces ashore on hostile coasts. However, achieving that objective has changed dramatically. Greek, Roman, or Viking raiders would sail their galleys or long ships onto a beach and then simply jump ashore, before charging at the enemy.

Today's amphibious forces have to operate in a far more sophisticated way and a successful amphibious landing involves many complex and inter-related activities.

An amphibious force comprises several elements and they all have specific tasks that each require specialist training and equipment.

A key task that needs to be undertaken thoroughly before troops can be launched ashore is

RIGHT: Amphibious warriors need to be at home on land, sea and in the air. (MOD/CROWN COPYRIGHT)

beach reconnaissance. It is vital that amphibious commanders have accurate information on the state of the shore line before they launch boats or landing craft towards a beach. It is essential that commanders know about the presence of underwater rocks or soft sand that is impassable to vehicles so they can re-direct their assault force in a different direction or employ specialist engineers to clear a safe route.

Beach reconnaissance teams also need to identify enemy defences close to landing sites so they can be neutralised by naval gunfire or air strikes before the landing force comes ashore. If the enemy has positioned strong defence along shore lines, then amphibious commanders may well decide to land their troops in a different location.

A key element of a successful amphibious landing is achieving surprise, so the enemy are caught unawares and have no idea they are about to be attacked. For this reason, any beach reconnaissance effort needs to be conducted covertly so as not to alert the enemy that it is underway. Only highly trained elite troops, such as the British Special Boat Service (SBS), or US Navy SEALS, are used for these tasks. They have to be trained to use underwater craft, scuba gear or kayaks to approach the enemy

coast undetected and then be able to return safely with their vital intelligence.

The main assault amphibious contingent is often called the landing force and they are usually combat units of infantry, which are armed and equipped to enable them to rapidly move inland and begin engaging the enemy's main land units. Most armed force designate the units in the landing force as marines and these are often units with long

traditions of operating from ships, stretching back centuries.

Landing forces are usually provided with artillery, armoured vehicles, and logistic support vehicles. These need to be designed to be loaded onto landing ships and then be able to drive across beaches after moving off the ramps of landing craft. Modifications for amphibious operations include the elevation of exhaust pipes so they do not let water into the vehicle's engine.

ABOVE: Once ashore, Royal Marines get ready to push inland. (MOD/CROWN COPYRIGHT)

BELOW: Hovercraft have added a new dimension to amphibious warfare. Here the Russian Navy's Zubr-class LCAC's, RFS *Mordovia* and RFS *Yevgeniy Kocheshkov* take part in an exercise in Kaliningrad. (RUSSIAN MINISTRY OF DEFENCE/ ALEEY KITAYEV)

Amphibious commanders need to be able to use multiple options to get their landing force ashore depending on the tactical scenario, so their equipment needs to flexible enough to be either loaded on a landing craft or under-slung beneath a helicopter. This means amphibious forces often have towed artillery pieces or wheeled armoured vehicles, rather than heavy tracked armoured vehicles.

In World War Two, the first tracked amphibious armoured vehicles were used and modern versions are used by many marine units. These can be launched from landing ships and then 'swim' ashore to carry a squad of infantry to their objectives inland. However, helicopters have transformed amphibious warfare over the past 70 years. They allow parts of the landing force to be put ashore in-land from the coast, allowing them to bypass enemy beach defences. This in turns reduces the vulnerability of landing crafts and boats and improves the chances of achieving surprise. It also means that the main amphibious flotilla can operate further out at sea, reducing their vulnerability to enemy coastal defence gun and missile batteries. Once the helicopter-borne troops have cleared a safe beach, or captured a port, follow-on landing forces can be brought ashore in relative safety. The introduction of helicopters has relegated D-Day style direct beach assaults under fire to history.

Once the landing force has secured its beachhead ashore, to keep it fighting, the logistic support force needs to swing into action to keep supplies of ammunition, fuel, and food flowing to the frontline. This also requires specialist troops and equipment.

First, engineering units need to move ashore to install roadways on beaches to ensure heavy logistic vehicles do not get stuck on soft sand trying to get off beaches, after disembarking from landing craft. The engineers also need to have bulldozers and other plant to clear

obstacles or routes off beaches, as well as neutralising minefields.

To keep the flow of supplies moving, specialist cargo handling equipment needs to be installed in ships and landing craft. Conditions on beaches can change rapidly as tides rise and fall, so beach command teams need to have specialist recovery vehicles that can quickly swing into action to pull bogged down vehicles out of trouble.

Building up combat power on beachheads can be slow, so the landing force needs specialist teams who are able to rapidly call-in fire support from warships cruising off shore, attack helicopters, or strike jets. These fire controllers need to be highly trained and very fit to be able to carry and operate their heavy and cumbersome target locating and communications equipment in very demanding environments and terrain.

Choreographing all the elements of an amphibious force requires highly trained and experienced commanders. Command arrangements need to be very clear cut and easily understood by all the troops and units taking part in any landing and to ensure this a single overall amphibious commander is usually appointed. Specific subordinates are responsible for delivery of the landing force ashore. Once on land, a ground commander is responsible for fighting the enemy. Another commander is responsible for logistic support. All these commanders and their staff need

to be well drilled on handing over control of units and personnel as they progress from ship to shore.

Amphibious forces also have great utility in situations other than all-out war. They can be manoeuvred close to crisis zones and then be held offshore ready to intervene at the direction of their governments. These include the evacuation of embassies or civilians threatened by hostiles forces or civil unrest. In extreme situations, the amphibious forces need to be able to fight their way ashore and then safely extract themselves.

Relief operations after natural disasters and humanitarian crisis are also well suited to the employment of amphibious forces, particularly their specialist shipping. Landing ships, landing craft, and assault helicopters can be rapidly dispatched to disaster zones and then move large amounts of aid ashore in situations where ports and other communications links have been devastated.

Amphibious forces are powerful and flexible assets for the nations that have them. They are designed to operate in complex and challenging environments and tactical situations.

ABOVE: Fast raiding craft are ideal for patrolling in littoral waters. (MOD/CROWN COPYRIGHT)

BELOW: Landing craft crews are often marines rather than sailors, giving them a strong bond with the troops they have to put ashore. (MOD/CROWN COPYRIGHT)

Disaster at Gallipoli

The Dardanelles Landings

RIGHT: No amount of heroism by the assault troops could compensate for the flawed execution of an over ambitious plan.

By the end of 1914, the war on the Western Front in France was bogged down into the stalemate of trench warfare. The frontline barely moved and hundreds of thousands of soldiers died in futile attacks. They were mown down by machine gun fire, blasted by artillery fire, and left dying on barbed wire entanglements. Government and military commanders were desperate to find a way to break the stalemate and Britain's First Lord of the Admiralty, Winston Churchill, pushed for a campaign to knock Germany's ally, the Ottoman Empire, out of the war. His intention was to capture its capital, Istanbul and the initial idea was to launch a naval flotilla through the Dardanelles straits, to bombard Istanbul and then land 80,000 troops to capture the city.

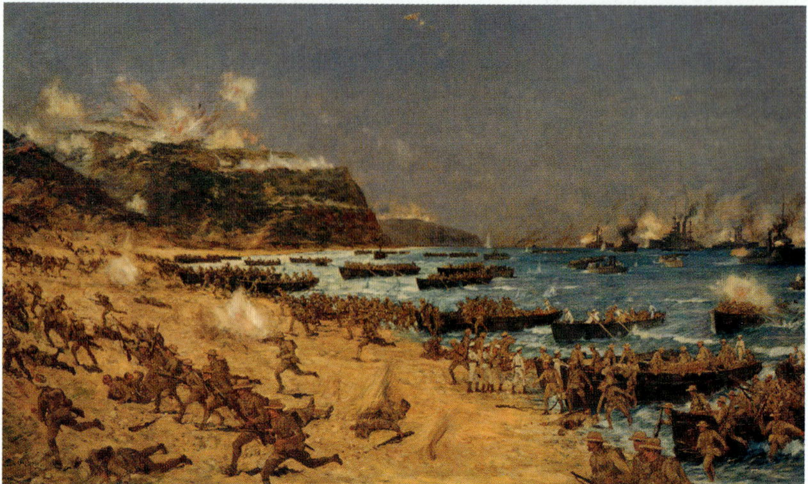

The invasion force, of French and British Empire troops, gathered in Egypt in the first months of 1915 and, in early March, the naval armada began its attack. British and French battleships tried to force their way through the Dardanelles on March 15, but they ran into a network

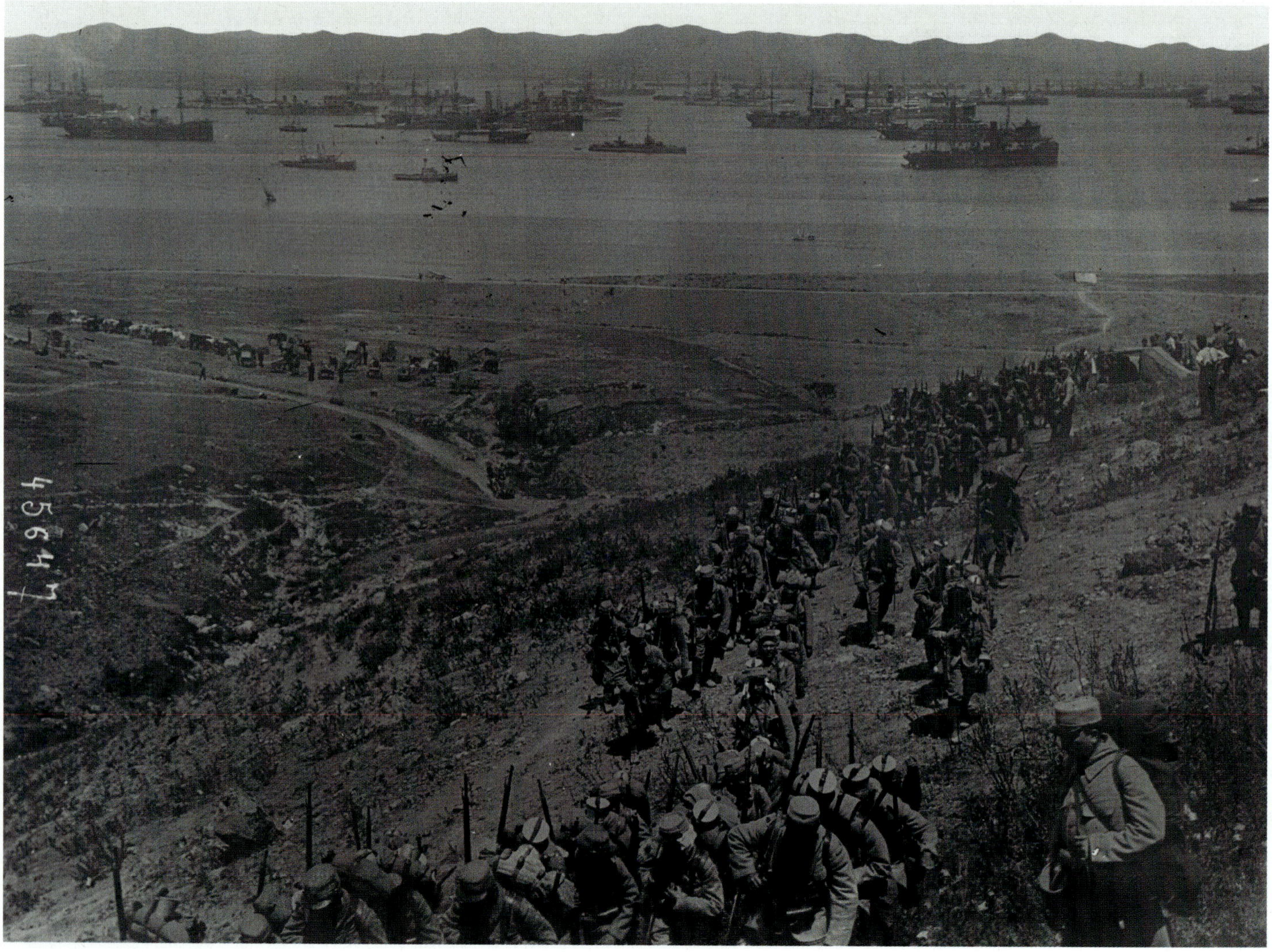

BELOW: Allied troops, including a strong contingent of French soldiers, were part of the initial wave ashore on the Dardanelles. (ARCHIVES NEW ZEALAND)

The Allied troops never managed to move much further inland, despite several attempts. For the rest of the year, the Allied and Turkish troops were locked into a brutal trench battle that resembled that on the Western Front. In October, it was apparent that the campaign was doomed, and preparations were made to withdraw the Allied troops. The final troops were lifted off the beaches on January 9, 2016.

Despite its high hopes, the campaign was a bloody failure. More than 57,000 British Empire and French troops were killed, and 240,000 Allied soldiers were wounded. Turkish losses were almost as bad, with 56,000 killed and nearly 200,000 wounded.

The whole Dardanelles campaign was a textbook illustration of how not to conduct amphibious operations. Surprise was lost, the enemy were well prepared, the landing force was not equipped to move rapidly ashore and once it landed it was unable to quickly move inland.

LEFT: After the failure of the initial landings, the fighting soon bogged down into trench warfare. (MITCHELL LIBRARY, STATE LIBRARY OF NEW SOUTH WALES)

BOTTOM: The lack of specialist landing craft prevented the troops getting ashore on the Dardanelles in a speedy fashion. (LIEUTENANT REGINALD ARTHUR SAVORY)

BELOW: ANZAC Cove was the famous landing beach of the Australian New Zealand Army Corps. (AUSTRALIAN WAR MEMORIAL)

of minefields. Six battleships hit mines and three sank with heavy losses. A recall order was issued.

A new plan was devised for an invasion force to land on the Dardanelles peninsula to capture the headlands overlooking the passage north to Istanbul and from there to march north to the city. On paper, the plan looked viable, but in the month that it took the invasion force to be re-assembled, the Turks were able to reinforce and fortify the beaches and cliffs overlooking the Dardanelles.

The invasion force appeared off the Dardanelles on April 25 and the troops started disembarking from passenger liners into whaling boats and other small craft to row themselves ashore. Unfortunately, the Turks were well prepared for the attack and as the invasion force came ashore it was mercilessly raked by artillery and machine gun fire. Casualties were horrendous.

Some contingents were landed on the wrong beaches, which were not heavily defended, but the commanders had little idea where they were or what was going on elsewhere in the operation. As result they failed to exploit their success and troops did not move inland.

The troops that managed to get ashore fought like lions, with the Lancashire Fusiliers famously winning five Victoria Crosses for gallantry 'before breakfast'. The Australian and New Zealand Army Corps, or ANZAC, troops met fierce resistance and lost 2,000 men within hours of going ashore.

By the end of the first day, the Turks had managed to contain all the landings and the assault troops started to dig-in to protect their exposed positions from enemy artillery fire. In many cases, the

Allied troops were perched on the edge of cliff tops and their positions were all overlooked by the Turkish artillery spotters.

Stuck on the Beach

Operation Jubilee at Dieppe

ABOVE: The iconic image of the defeat at Dieppe. Thousands of Canadian troops were pinned down on the beaches by well motivated and organised German defenders. (IMPERIAL WAR MUSEUM)

After the British Expeditionary Force (BEF) was evacuated from Dunkirk in June 1940, Prime Minister Winston Churchill ordered plans to be made to strike back against Nazi occupied Europe.

A force of elite raiding troops, dubbed the Commandos after the highly effective Boer forces, was set up and it was overseen by the newly established Combined Operations Headquarters. The first Commando raid against Norway took place in March 1941, and over the following year more complex raids were conducted.

Lord Louis Mountbatten, the chief of Combined Operations, wanted to build experience of amphibious operations ahead of the launch of the eventual Anglo-American invasion of mainland Europe. By the early summer of 1942, the Russians were pushing the British and Americans to launch the second front in the west

to take the pressure off their troops on the eastern front. The bulk of the available US and British forces were

RIGHT: The head of Combined Operations. Lord Louis Mountbatten oversaw Operation Jubilee. (ALLAN WARREN)

directed to land in North Africa later in 1942, so a large raid was ordered against the coast of France. The idea was to boost morale and try to divert German troops from the conflict with Russia.

The 2nd Canadian Infantry Division was assigned to carry out Operation Jubilee, supported by several hundred British and French Commandos and 50 US Army Rangers. It was intended to land the assault force at Dieppe and capture the French fishing port. Then, after demolishing port infrastructure and German coastal defences, the raiding force was to be withdrawn. A large force of Royal Air Force fighters was to support the raid and hopefully draw the German Luftwaffe into action, inflicting heavy losses on them.

Operation Jubilee got underway in the early hours of August 19, 1942, with operations by the Commando units to seize and destroy German gun batteries on

the cliffs overlooking the port, to the north and south of the town. It fell to the Canadian troops to make the main assault on Dieppe, landing along the length of the town's beach. They were to be supported by 58 Churchill tanks, which had the task of knocking out German machine gun bunkers, allowing the infantry to get off the beach and onto the promenade, before moving into the town.

However, although the first landing craft got to the beach and landed the first wave of Canadian troops safely, the landing craft carrying the tanks were delayed. Eventually only 29 of the 58 got ashore and soon even 14 of those were bogged down in soft sand. The Germans were now fully alerted, and their machine guns and mortars were raking the beach. Hundreds of Canadians were already dead or wounded.

Just 15 tanks managed to get off the beach onto the promenade, but they were soon blocked from moving further inland by a network of concrete tank obstacles.

By 9.40am, it was clear that the main assault force was not going to be able to get off the beaches and a withdrawal was signalled. Royal Navy warships started to generate a smoke screens to cover the retreat as landing craft were sent in to pick up the remaining troops. The last survivors recovered were lifted off just before 2pm and the raid was then declared over.

Out of the 5,000-strong Canadian contingent, 3,367 were killed, wounded, or taken prisoner, which represented a casualty rate of 68%. The 1,000 strong British Commando force lost 247 men while less than 350 German troops were killed in the course of the brief battle.

Operation Jubilee was a disaster. The assault was not able to penetrate the German defences and get off the beaches. However, the outcome was instrumental in the decisions to develop the specialist engineering and swimming, or Duplex Drive (DD), tanks that proved so successful on D-Day. It was an expensive way to learn a lesson, with the 2nd Canadian Infantry Division losing nearly half of its combat troops.

ABOVE: German troops rounded up hundreds of Canadians who could not make their escape after the withdrawal was ordered. (IMPERIAL WAR MUSEUM)

LEFT: Royal Navy landing craft ventured into the beaches on the morning of August 19 to bring off the surviving Canadian troops. (IMPERIAL WAR MUSEUM)

Raising the Stars and Stripes

US Marines in the Pacific

RIGHT: **Hit the Beach. The first wave of US Marines land on Iwo Jima in the face of fanatical Japanese resistance.** (US NATIONAL ARCHIVES)

The US Marine Corps 'island-hopping' campaign in the Pacific during World War Two saw some of the biggest amphibious operations ever undertaken and led to major tactical innovations.

The US Marine Corps is one of the oldest American military units, tracing its history back to the Revolutionary wars in 1775. The corps then took part in several famous expeditions to protect American trade and establish what would eventually become the United States overseas territories, or colonies, in Cuba and the Philippines.

It was only in the 1920s that the USMC began to think seriously about developing a modern amphibious warfare doctrine. Young officers, including Major Earl 'Pete' Ellis, had studied British and ANZAC experiences at Gallipoli and were instrumental in developing ideas about how to conduct amphibious landings against well prepared enemy defences - in the era of aircraft carriers, long range bombers and submarines. Marine Corps leaders identified that America's main enemy would be Japan if another global war should break out and much of the conflict would revolve around the control of key islands in the centre of the Pacific. America would have to be able to control these islands to allow the establishment of air and naval

bases, which could eventually be used to strike at the Japanese homeland.

The concept of the Fleet Marine Force was developed from 1934 and this envisaged the establishment of permanent units trained for amphibious operations, supported by purpose-built landing craft and amphibious assault ships that could operate across the expanse of the Pacific. Development began of the Amphibious Vehicle, Tracked, or LVT, also known as the Alligator, armoured

BELOW: **US Navy aircraft carriers provided vital air support during the island-hopping campaign across the Pacific.** (US NATIONAL ARCHIVES)

LEFT: Pacific islands were surrounded by coral reefs, so the US Marines needed the tracked Alligators to move over them to get ashore.
(US NATIONAL ARCHIVES)

tractor to carry squads of marines off ships and drive over the coral reefs that surrounded many Pacific islands.

A dedicated amphibious training centre was set up and USMC units were rotated through it to build experience and expertise. Regimental combat teams (RCT), trained and equipped for amphibious assaults, were set up in both the Atlantic and Pacific fleets. As well as infantry elements, each RCT also contained light artillery, logistic troops, engineers, anti-aircraft, and signal communication troops, so they could operate independently. From 1935, a series of Fleet Landing Exercises were held to trial these new ideas. In June 1941, the Amphibious Corps consisting of the 1st Marine Division, the 1st Army Division, marine and army air components, commanded by a USMC Major General Holland Smith, was set up. He would later command several of the most important amphibious assaults during the war in the Pacific. At the heart of the Amphibious Corps concept was the integration of air, land, and naval forces under a single commander to ensure battlefield success.

The US Marines put their amphibious warfare doctrine to the test on a large scale for the first time during the Guadalcanal campaign in the summer and autumn of 1942, when they were sent to seize the southern Solomon Islands. This saw the 1st Marine Division sail from New Zealand to land on Guadalcanal in August 1942. It did not have much

of the new equipment and specialist shipping so still relied largely on open top motor boats to come ashore from converted troop transports.

The US assault was put ashore on largely undefended beaches and the main force moved rapidly to capture an airfield on the island. USMC Grumman Wildcat fighter bombers were soon flown in, and they then provided vital air cover when the Japanese launched a massive counter-attack to try to overrun the US

enclave. The marines survived weeks of human wave attacks by hundreds of Japanese infantry. USMC artillery and the Wildcats drove off the Japanese and the US won its first land victory of the war in the region.

By the following year, the Americans were taking the offensive in the central Pacific in their drive towards Japan. The first island to be assaulted by the US Marines was Tarawa in November, which was defended by 5,000 Japanese ➤

BELOW: Alligator amphibious tractors brought the first US Marines ashore on Pacific islands, providing fire power to defeat Japanese beach defences.
(US NATIONAL ARCHIVES)

ABOVE: Large landing ships carried tanks and other heavy vehicles on to beaches to help the US Marines move inland.
(US NATIONAL ARCHIVES)

yet when they stormed Iwo Jima. More than 22,000 Japanese were dug in on the island when 70,000 marines of the V Amphibious Corps attacked, under the command of General Holland.

A huge air and naval bombardment preceded the assault, but the Japanese had dug themselves so deep underground that only a handful were killed or injured before the landings commenced. The marines came ashore on February 19 and immediately found themselves under heavy machine gun and artillery fire. In the first day of the battle the marines had lost 2,000 killed or wounded. Four days after the initial landing, the marines reached the summit of Mount Suribachi in the heart of island and planted the stars and stripes. The

defenders who were dug into deep bunkers and surrounded by minefields. By this time much of the Marines' specialist equipment and new shipping had been brought on stream but the Japanese were prepared, and only extensive use of naval gunfire and air support neutralised the defenders. It took the Americans three days to clear the island and when the battle was over only 17 Japanese were captured alive.

As the American island-hopping offensive continued the Japanese put up determined resistance so larger and larger assault forces were needed. The success of the amphibious campaign depended on the organisational skill of the US Navy to pre-load ships with marines, equipment and supplies at the home ports on the west coast of America or Hawaii, before the long voyage to the combat zone. 'Combat trains' of supply ships kept the marines on shore fully stocked with ammunition, food, and fuel.

By February 1945, the US Marines embarked on their toughest test

RIGHT: Japanese defenders put up fanatical resistance on the slopes of Mount Suribachi at the heart of Iwo Jima, so the US Marine brought up field guns to fire into enemy bunkers at near point blank range to flush them out.
(US NATIONAL ARCHIVES)

scene was immortalised in the famous photograph by Joe Rosenthal. It took another month to clear the remaining Japanese but this time more than 1,000 surrendered.

The finale of the American drive on Japan was Operation Iceberg to capture the island of Okinawa, just 500 kilometres from the Japanese mainland. This required a 180,000-strong American invasion force, made up of the US Marines V Amphibious Corps and US Army soldiers, under the command of the 10th US Army. More than 70,000 Japanese troops and tens of thousands of armed civilians were dug-in to defend the island. To protect the island the Japanese deployed 5,500 kamikaze, suicide aircraft in a bid to destroy the American fleet carrying the assault force.

In a change of tactics, the Japanese decided not to defend the shore line, so the American landing force was able to get ashore on April 1, 1945, with relatively few losses. Once they pushed inland, the Japanese staged huge counter-attacks that were only blunted by mass artillery fire and air strikes. It took more than two months of heavy fighting to clear Okinawa, and the last resistance was recorded on July 2. American losses were 49,451, including 12,520 dead or missing and 36,631 wounded. The Japanese lost approximately 110,000 killed, and 7,400 taken prisoner.

Operation Iceberg was the most demanding US amphibious operation of the Pacific campaign, and it is all the more remarkable because it was begun even before resistance ended on Iwo Jiwa. The

LEFT: US Marines made extensive use of flame throwers to kill Japanese troops inside heavily fortified bunkers across Iwo Jima. (US NATIONAL ARCHIVES)

near simultaneous execution of two massive amphibious operations, on the far side of the Pacific, was testament to the organisational ability of the US Navy and US Marines Corps to marshal amphibious forces on a scale never seen before.

BELOW: After the US Marines established their bridgehead on Okinawa, a huge logistic operation swung into action to keep them supplied with ammunition, food, and fuel. (US NATIONAL ARCHIVES)

D-Day Victory

The Longest Day in Normandy

ABOVE: The Atlantic Wall defences included the installation of obstacles along the Normandy beaches, which were designed to puncture the hulls of landing craft. (BUNDESARCHIVE)

In June 1944 France had been occupied by Nazi troops for four years. To defend his Third Reich, Adolf Hitler ordered a huge line of fortification to be built from the Spanish border to Denmark. He called it the Atlantic Wall.

Behind the beach fortification, elite panzer, or armoured, divisions were positioned ready to counterattack against any Allied landings. The Germans hoped to repeat the defeat of the Canadians at Dieppe.

In London, Allied military commanders and intelligence analysts worked for years to study the Atlantic Wall, looking for weaknesses and devising plans to break it apart. The lessons of Dieppe were taken on board by a joint planning team of British, American, and other Allied officers.

D-Day, as the landing was code-named, would be the largest amphibious operation ever undertaken, with 135,000 Allied troops being put ashore and a further 22,000 landing in France by parachute or glider. Normandy was selected because it was within range of Allied air cover, but crucially the Atlantic Wall's defences were not as thick as they were in the Pas de Calais region, opposite Dover at the narrowest point of the English Channel. To convince the Germans that the Allied landing would take place

RIGHT: The iconic image of the 'Longest Day', as the D-Day landings were soon nicknamed following a comment made by an aide to the German commander in Normandy, Erwin Rommel. (US NATIONAL ARCHIVES)

at the Pas de Calais, a major deception operation was launched, with dummy tanks and fake radio messages being used. In the days and weeks before D-Day, Allied bombing and sabotage attacks were directed to northeastern France to add to the fake impression.

To deliver the Allied armies to France, a huge naval armada was assembled in British ports. Operation Neptune, as the naval phase was codenamed, involved eight different navies, and comprised 6,939 vessels: 1,213 warships, 4,126 landing craft of various types, 736 ancillary craft, and 864 merchant vessels.

The invasion was originally scheduled for June 5, but bad weather prompted the supreme Allied commander, US Army General Dwight D Eisenhower to delay for a day.

During the afternoon and evening of June 5, the naval force set sail and the aircraft carrying the paratroopers took off for their drop zones. The first airborne troops landed just after midnight to seize key bridges to block German counterattacks on the invasion beaches. A fleet of mine sweepers cleared lanes through the minefields to allow landing ships to bring the invasion force to its unloading areas.

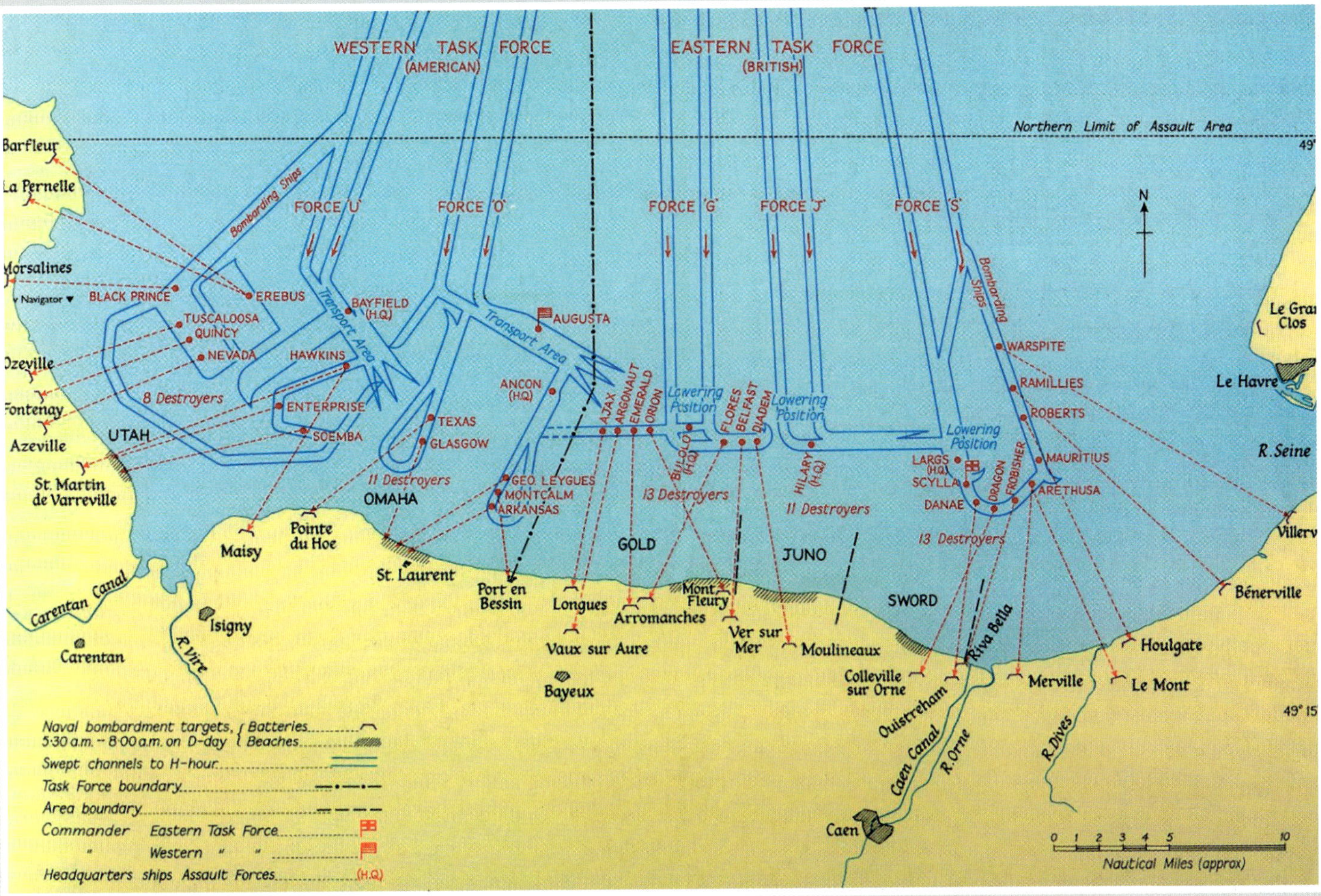

Along the length of the Normandy coast, German troops caught sight of the thousands of Allied ships off shore. They did not have long to take in the sight before the Allied battleships started to pound the Atlantic Wall.

Now the invasion troops started to scramble down the side of their troop ships into the landing craft that would carry them ashore. Nearby, on dozens of tank landing ships 176 Duplex-Drive, or DD, tanks were being drive off their open ramps. The DD tanks had a raised screen that created buoyancy and allowed the tanks to float. An extra-drive mechanism connected the tank's engines to propellers so they could move through water. The idea was

ABOVE: Allied naval commanders formulated a complex plan to deliver the Allied armies to Normandy and position battleships offshore to delivering fire support against German defences. (HMSO)

Huge gun emplacements were built along the Atlantic Wall by the Germans. (JEBULON)

for the DD tanks to hit the beach at the same time as the landing craft carrying the infantry, to provide armoured support as they cleared beach obstacles and then moved inland.

The Allies divided the landing zone into five beaches, with the British and American forces taking two beaches each, leaving the final one to the Canadians.

The most easterly beach was code-named Sword, and the British 3rd Infantry Division was given the task of capturing it. They then had to press inland to link up with the British 6th Airborne Division, who had landed ahead to capture bridges over the River Orne.

Next to them was Juno Beach, where the 3rd Canadian Division was to come ashore and head toward Caen, the largest city in Normandy. To the west of the Canadians was the British 50th (Northumbrian) Infantry Division on Gold Beach and its job was to press inland to link up with the nearby US troops.

The British and Canadian landings went largely to plan. Almost all their DD tanks got safely ashore and allowed the infantry to quickly breach the Atlantic Wall. Special flame thrower tanks, known as Crocodiles, and engineering tanks, dubbed AVREs, put German pill boxes out of action and dropped bundles of logs called fascines into anti-tank ditches to create routes for vehicles off the beaches. By midday troops from Sword Beach had linked up with the airborne units on the River Orne. British anti-tank guns and fighter bombers drove off a German tank attack in the afternoon, fully securing the British bridgeheads.

In the west of Normandy, the US 4th Infantry Division also managed to get ashore successfully on Utah Beach. Its 21 DD tanks all landed successfully, covering US engineers as they blew paths through the metal obstacles blocking the exits from the beach. By mid-morning, the 4th Division was pushing inland to link up with the paratroopers of the 82nd and 101st Airborne Divisions. Out of 21,000 US troops who landed on Utah Beach, only 197 were killed or wounded.

However, between Utah and Gold Beaches, was Omaha Beach. It was defended by the bulk of the German 352nd Infantry Division and this unit put up determined resistance to the US 29th Infantry Division as it tried to come ashore. Its landing was plagued by bad

RIGHT: Bloody Omaha. US troops approach Omaha Beach on June 6. They soon ran into heavy resistance from German defenders. (US NATIONAL ARCHIVES)

RIGHT: As the invasion fought their way off the beaches, the Allied navies started to deliver the next wave of reinforcements. (IMPERIAL WAR MUSEUM)

BELOW: British troops secured Gold Beach with relative ease and were soon pushing inland. (IMPERIAL WAR MUSEUM)

luck from the start. US bombers that were supposed to soften up the German defences dropped their ordnance short so when the first wave of landing craft dropped their ramps, they were raked by German machine gun fire. Rough seas swamped 27 of the 32 DD tanks that were supposed to accompany the assault troops. The five surviving tanks soon bogged down and never made it ashore.

On the beaches, the 29th Infantry Division's troops were on their own. It was a slaughter. The GIs were pinned down, with little cover and were soon taking heavy casualties. This episode was immortalised in the movie, *Saving Private Ryan*. By mid-morning, a flotilla of destroyers closed with the shore and started give fire support. This gave the Americans the covering fire they needed to blow holes in the barricades blocking routes off the beach. Hundreds of American troops now penetrated the German defences and started to clear them out of their bunkers. A follow-up wave of landing craft now brought reinforcements ashore, including tanks, and they were pushing inland by late afternoon. The battle for 'Bloody Omaha' cost the US Army 2,400 killed, wounded, or missing. It was the biggest single loss for an Allied division on D-Day.

Despite the heavy losses suffered on Omaha Beach, by the end of D-Day

the Allied invasion force was firmly ashore in France. More than 140,000 Allied troops had been landed, backed up by tanks and artillery. The airborne troops had prevented German counterattacks striking at the bridgehead. Nearly 10,000 Allied troops had been lost, including more than 4,000 killed, but the Germans had not been able to disrupt the invasion.

Over the next month more than 850,000 Allied troops were ashore

and, by the end of July, the German army in Normandy had been surrounded at Falaise. On August 19 Paris rose in the revolt against the German garrison and within a week Free French troops were driving into the city.

The largest amphibious operation in military history had successfully established a bridgehead in occupied Europe opening the way for the ultimate liberation of the continent.

ABOVE: US troops got safely ashore on Utah Beach and moved inland quickly to link up with American airborne troops. (US NATIONAL ARCHIVES)

BELOW: In the weeks after D-Day the race was on to bring in reinforcements to defeat the German panzer divisions, which were massing inland to counter-attack against the Normandy bridgehead. (US NATIONAL ARCHIVES)

Operation Corporate 1982

Britain's Falklands Assault

In April 1982, Britain dispatched a Royal Navy task force to the South Atlantic to re-capture the Falkland Islands from Argentine troops who had occupied the territory the previous month.

The task force under Rear Admiral Sandy Woodward, was able to sink Argentina's only battleship and send the rest of the South American fleet back to port for the remainder of the conflict. However, the British government was not willing to authorise attacks on the Argentine mainland to neutralise the Argentine air force, so Woodward needed to develop a plan to successfully land the amphibious troops of 3 Commando Brigade without air supremacy.

As the British gathered more intelligence on Argentine troop deployments and gained experience of operating around the Falklands, it became clear that the best site to put a British landing force ashore was in San Carlos Water. This bay, which split into two smaller bays, provided shelter to allow landing craft to move troops and equipment ashore and it was also surrounded by high hills, where anti-aircraft missile batteries could be sited. Crucially, there were only a few Argentine outposts around the bay, and they had not prepared the area for defence.

During the evening of May 19, Woodward received final authorisation from the War Cabinet in London to proceed with Operation Sutton, as the landing was codenamed. He decided to start the operation the following evening, with the troops set to land on the Falklands by dawn on May 21.

On the eve of the landings, HMS *Antrim* dispatched its helicopter to insert a Special Boat Squadron (SBS) assault team to neutralise a small Argentine observation post on Fanning Head, at the entrance to San Carlos Water.

The scene was now set for the largest British amphibious operation since World War Two.

Woodward was fearful that the fully loaded amphibious shipping could be exposed to Argentine Exocet missile and air attack if they approached the Falklands in daylight. So, he ordered the ships to approach under cover of darkness and for the

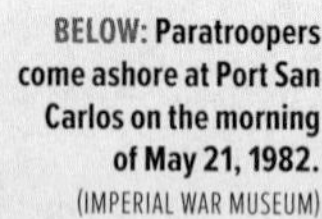

first troops to go ashore at 2.30am, giving them only a couple of hours of darkness to cover their initial landing. One destroyer and seven frigates would be positioned as a 'gun line' in Falkland Sound to defend the amphibious fleet - two assault ships, seven fleet auxiliary ships, and three commandeered merchant ships - as they were unloading the landing force in San Carlos Water. The hills around the landing beaches would prevent the Argentines using their Exocet missiles to take out any of the large ships carrying hundreds of troops. Hopefully, the bulk of the troops would be ashore long before the Argentines realised what was happening and could mobilise their air force to attack.

The morning of May 21 proved to be anticlimactic for the British. Surprise was complete.

SBS officers started off the action by calling down 4.5-inch naval gunfire from HMS *Antrim* onto the Argentine position on Fanning Head. Nine of the Argentine contingent were killed or captured. The remaining troops fled into the night and had a long walk back to their base.

The assault ships, HMS *Fearless* and HMS *Intrepid,* were the first to enter San Carlos Water because their 16 landing craft had to quickly move out of their well decks to start

ABOVE: San Carlos Water seen from Sussex Mountain. It was a natural anchorage and was selected because it provided protection from South Atlantic storms and Argentine air attacks.
(IMPERIAL WAR MUSEUM)

LEFT: Royal Marines captured stragglers from the Argentine outpost on Fanning Point on the morning of May 21, 1982.
(IMPERIAL WAR MUSEUM)

collecting troops from other ships of the amphibious fleet. As dawn was breaking the first soldiers of 2nd Battalion, Parachute Regiment went ashore at the southern edge of San Carlos Water. Minutes later, Royal Marines of 40 Commando were put ashore near San Carlos Settlement. They were subsequently joined by 45 Commando.

Other major units followed during the day, with 3rd Battalion, Parachute Regiment and 42 Commando landing around Port San Carlos. Once the fighting troops were ashore, the landing craft and Mexeflote pontoons started to land 3 Commando Brigade's logistic equipment, stores, and ammunition.

The 42-strong Argentine garrison at San Carlos Settlement was not attacked before dawn. Its soldiers were still in position when the liner *Canberra* arrived offshore, and they had a grandstand view of British troops being unloaded into landing craft at 8.10am. The Argentine commander decided to retreat but quickly radioed his superior officers about what he had seen. The British had now lost the element of surprise.

As the Argentine troops withdrew, they engaged a low flying British Gazelle utility helicopter whose pilot did not realise there were enemy troops in the area. The helicopter crashed in the bay and one crewman later died of his injuries. He was the only British fatality on land during Operation Sutton.

At their airbases in southern Argentina, the country's air force and navy pilots had been preparing for this day for almost two months. The Argentine pilots pressed home their low-level strikes against the British ships with great bravery. Television news footage showed the Argentine jets appearing to weave through the masts of British ships as anti-aircraft shells exploded around them.

In the end, the bravery of the Argentine pilots would not change the course of the battle. Poor planning, unserviceable aircraft, bad weather, bomb fuses that did not work, long distances and most crucially a lack of precise intelligence on the location and type of British ships meant that only a fraction of Argentine aircraft could drop their bombs anywhere near any type of target. Only a handful of the bombs that were dropped actually did any serious damage to British ships.

The Argentine attack plan involved launching several waves of between 10 and 20 aircraft during the day in the hope of overwhelming the British defences. After air-to-air refuelling en route to the Falklands, the Argentine jets made their final approach at low-level over West Falkland before swooping across Falkland Sound on their final attack run. The Argentine jets were armed with iron, or dumb, bombs which meant they had to overfly their targets before releasing their weapons. To try to smooth the way to their targets the Argentine pilots opened fire with their cannons. It required strong nerves and considerable skill to actually get a bomb on target.

The Argentine air force was first into action late on the morning of May 21 when a formation of 12 Dassault Daggers made an appearance over Falkland Sound. Flights of three jets broke up to strike at HMS *Argonaut*, HMS *Broadsword*, HMS *Antrim,* and HMS *Brilliant*. They managed to drop nine bombs but only one hit its target, HMS *Antrim*. The big destroyer was badly damaged by cannon fire from the jets and eventually had to take cover in San Carlos Water to carry out repairs. Other ships had close shaves as bombs exploded around them. The British surface-to-air missiles again proved temperamental with only one missile hitting a Dagger. The rest of the Argentine jets returned safely to base.

This set the scene for the rest of the day. Eleven more formations of more than 60 Argentine jets were launched into action but just over half were able to make attack runs and dropped just

44 bombs between them. Out of those, only eight hit their targets and then only half exploded.

It fell to the Royal Navy Sea Harriers to inflict the most damage on the Argentine pilots, shooting down nine of their jets – five Skyhawks and four Daggers – during the day. Except in one incident when three Daggers were intercepted approaching Falkland Sound, all the Argentine aircraft were shot down as they escaped after dropping their bombs.

This success came at a cost. HMS *Ardent* was lost after four bombs detonated on her. HMS *Antrim* and

HMS *Argonaut* had unexploded bombs inside. Both HMS *Broadsword* and HMS *Brilliant* had been badly damaged by cannon fire.

The warships protecting the amphibious landing had taken a heavy pounding, but the Argentine pilots had made a major tactical error in concentrating on attacking the 'gun line' in Falkland Sound, rather than striking the amphibious ships in San Carlos Water. This allowed more than 3,000 troops to get ashore with over 1,000 tons of supplies. The British were firmly ashore on the Falklands and would not be expelled.

ABOVE: Once secure in the bridgehead at San Carlos, the Royal Marines and Paratroopers of 3 Commando Brigade started to march east towards Port Stanley. (IMPERIAL WAR MUSEUM)

LEFT: San Carlos Water was soon nicknamed 'Bomb Alley' by the crews of British ships who endured days of bombing by Argentine jets. (IMPERIAL WAR MUSEUM)

Al Faw Landing

Royal Marines Lead Invasion of Iraq

ABOVE: The northern Arabian Gulf was the venue for the first opposed British amphibious landing since the 1956 Suez crisis. The Operation Telic landings in Iraq were not as big as those on the Falklands in 1982, but no Argentine troops had resisted the landings at San Carlos. (MOD/CROWN COPYRIGHT)

In the early hours of March 20, 2003, a formation of British Chinook transport helicopters loaded with Royal Marine Commandos was approaching a landing zone on Iraq's Al Faw peninsula. This was the most southerly point of Iraqi territory, and it contained installations that were used to pump oil out to platforms in the northern Arabian Gulf, where it was loaded on tankers for export.

Coalition military planners wanted to seize the oil installations and then take control of all of the estuaries where the Euphrates and Tigris rivers flow into Gulf, as well as Iraq's main port at Umm Qasr. The region was low lying and made up mostly of salt marshes and swamps making it impossible for heavy armoured units to traverse. Britain's 3 Commando Brigade was given the mission of capturing Al Faw to prevent its oil infrastructure being sabotaged and then to dominate Iraq's littoral region, to open a route to Basra, the largest city in southern Iraq. The operation would open with the first opposed amphibious landing undertaken by British forces since the 1956 Suez campaign.

The invasion phase of Operation Telic eventually involved the deployment of two submarines, 17 warships, 14 Royal Fleet Auxiliary vessels, 45 Fleet Air Arm helicopters, and more than 8,000 Royal Navy sailors and 4,000 Royal Marine Commandos.

British Prime Minister Tony Blair ordered the Royal Navy and Royal Marines to the Middle East with the objective of disarming Iraq of its arsenal of weapons of mass destruction, which US and British intelligence said Saddam Hussein had hidden away in contravention of United Nations mandates. Eventually none of these infamous weapons were found, which added to the unpopularity of the war.

The Royal Navy task group moved into the Northern Arabian Gulf in the run up to the war, ready to launch the assault force in Royal Air Force and Royal Navy helicopters to seize Al Faw. Sea mines and mines on beaches meant a direct beach assault could not be contemplated until helicopter-landed troops had secured the landing sites. Once they had secured the southern tip of the peninsula, the landing craft and other helicopter

RIGHT: Royal Navy Sea King HC4s flew the first waves of Royal Marines on to the Al Faw peninsula from HMS *Ark Royal*. (MOD/CROWN COPYRIGHT)

were to bring ashore vehicles and supplies to support the Royal Marines as they advanced up the Al Faw towards Basra. The US Marines were to provide additional helicopters to lift the first wave of Royal Marines. A team of US Navy SEALS were to carry out a close reconnaissance of the Al Faw oil installations and direct a US Air Force Lockheed AC-130 Spectre gunship to provide fire support as the British Commandos landed.

In the days before the operation a large sandstorm swept into the northern Arabian Gulf, so the landing force and its transport helicopters was flown off the Royal Navy amphibious ships to a field site in Kuwait to escape the bad weather. When the assault force lifted off in the early hours of March 20, a US CH-46E Sea Knight crashed, killing eight British passengers and four US crew. The US command grounded all its helicopters, but the British decided to press ahead using their own.

First to land on Al Faw were 40 Commando, who disembarked from RAF Chinook HC2 heavy lift helicopters while under enemy fire. The Royal Marines soon overran the outnumbered Iraqi defenders, who were completely demoralised by the firepower of the Spectre gunship. Royal Navy frigates joined in the battle to neutralise the Iraqi artillery positions to the north with naval gunfire.

The Royal Marines then started advancing up the peninsula along the single road to Basra, which was built on a raised bank along the side of the Shatt -al-Arab waterway.

ABOVE: The Royal Marines of 40 Commando on the Al Faw received a non-stop flow of helicopters bringing in supplies as the operations continued. (MOD/CROWN COPYRIGHT)

BELOW: HMS *Ark Royal* was the flagship for the Royal Navy amphibious task group during the operation to seize the Al Faw peninsula. (TIM RIPLEY)

At dawn, another wave of helicopters from the fleet started to shuttle ashore reinforcements and supplies. Once mines had been cleared from the beaches by Royal Engineers, landing craft brought ashore the Scimitar light tanks of the Queen's Dragoon Guards.

On the western side of the Al Faw, another operation was underway to seize Umm Qasr port on the Khawr Abd Allah estuary. US Marines captured the port by driving directly from Kuwait and they soon handed it over to the Royal Marines, who turned it into a base for 539 Assault Squadron and 42 Commando to dominate the marshes of southern Afghanistan, using hovercraft, landing craft, and rigid raiders. Over the next three weeks, they duelled with small Iraqi detachments as the Royal Marine craft pushed up the Khawr

Abd Allah waterway to the port of Zubayr.

The Royal Marines then advanced up the Al Faw peninsula to the outskirts of Basra, including storming a heavily fortified Iraqi town south of the city. They were accompanied by a contingent of British Army Challenger 2 tanks that had been ferried across the Khawr Abd Allah on a ferry installed by the Royal Marines. This was the first time since Suez that the Royal Marines had operated with main battle tanks.

The Battle for Basra reached a climax in the first week of April when resistance to the British raids seemed to weaken. After American troops entered Baghdad, the British Army commander, Major General Robin Brims, ordered an all-out assault on Basra on April 6. Pushing into the city from the south, were the Royal Marines of 3 Commando Brigade, who had the objective of taking Saddam Hussein's Palace in

Basra. Crowds of cheering civilians met the British columns. Sixteen personnel from Royal Navy and 3 Commando Brigade had been killed during the invasion, all in helicopters crashes, friendly fire incidents, or from natural causes.

However, this honeymoon did not last long as the hungry and poverty-stricken citizens of Basra decided to take their revenge on the vestiges of Saddam's regime. Within days anarchy engulfed the city, public buildings were looted, and public utilities started to fail. Soon the city's power and water supplies collapsed, as the summer heat approached. The Royal Marines had to rapidly switch from war fighting mode into being peacekeepers and humanitarian workers, before 3 Commando Brigade was ordered home in May 2023.

The Al Faw operation was not a straightforward amphibious assault but a complex operation to dominate Iraq's littoral region. A mix of helicopters, landing craft, hovercraft, and raiding boats were used to insert and then support the Royal Marines as they advanced towards Basra. It provided a lessons on how amphibious forces have adapted to the changing nature of warfare in the 21st century.

LEFT: The campaign by the Royal Navy and Royal Marines in 2003 was a sign post to future amphibious operations in littoral regions. (MOD/CROWN COPYRIGHT)

BELOW: Royal Marine hovercrafts proved ideal for operating around the marshlands of southern Iraq. (MOD/CROWN COPYRIGHT)

Littoral Strike

Operating on the Waterfront

RIGHT: Small raiding craft are ideal for dominating coastal waters in littoral regions. (MOD/CROWN COPYRIGHT)

Amphibious landings conjure up images of swarms of landing craft coming ashore on D-Day, against a backdrop of huge expanses of sandy beaches. However, generations of amphibious commanders have learned the hard way that they need to be ready to send their forces into action in a wide variety of maritime environments.

Coastlines come in infinite varieties - beaches, rocky shoreline, coral reefs, island chains, river estuaries, marshes, and swamps. This zone between the deep ocean and the coast line is known in amphibious warfare jargon, as the littoral. It is not neatly defined but is generally referred to as the zone where ocean going vessels can't operate, requiring specialist craft to deliver amphibious forces to the shore. Enemy coastal defences are also likely to be active in littoral regions, enhancing the risks involved in sending amphibious forces and vessels into it.

The very first elements of amphibious forces to enter littoral zones are reconnaissance teams

BELOW: Covert insertion of beach reconnaissance teams by submarine are an essential precursor to amphibious landings. (MOD/CROWN COPYRIGHT)

looking to identify enemy positions and gain accurate information about environmental conditions. This is the age old need to conduct beach reconnaissance to find out if there are underwater rocks or coral reefs that could ground landing craft before then even get to the shore. Whether sand can take heavy vehicles, or if mines are to be found, it is vital information for amphibious planners. Time and again, the lesson has been learnt that there is no substitute for a real human being going ashore to collect this vital information. Charts and aerial photographs just do not cut it. This mission also needs to be done covertly so the enemy has no idea that an amphibious assault is being planned. The element of surprise is still a key element in successfully putting troops ashore, with minimal losses.

In World War Two, this highly dangerous mission was undertaken by the forefathers of the modern Special Boat Service (SBS) or US Navy SEALs. They had to swim ashore from submerged submarines using scuba gear, or rowing in canoes, to covertly land on enemy beaches and then return with this critical intelligence. Often these beach reconnaissance teams were given the additional task of planting demolition charges to destroy enemy defences to clear away for an amphibious assault.

In the modern era, beach reconnaissance teams have been provided with new ways of getting ashore, undetected. Many amphibious forces have given their beach reconnaissance units underwater craft known as swimmer delivery systems, or SDS. These not quite

a mini-submarine but are a vessel that divers can sit on for journeys of several kilometres to shore. This allows divers to take large quantities of oxygen with them so they can stay submerged for long periods, before they have to swim the final leg of their journey to the enemy held shore line. Submarines can be fitted with docks to carry SDS across oceans before they need to be launched.

Aerial delivery of beach reconnaissance teams is now also common. Helicopters provide long insert options, but they are noisy and can't fly to close to enemy territory to avoid alerting defenders. Another option is high altitude, low opening, or HALO, parachute insertion, which has the advantage of being silent and involves a high-flying aircraft that is

often out of view any defenders on the ground.

In situations short of all out war, amphibious forces are often called on to dominate littoral zones to protect shipping out in deeper water from attacks by pirates or terrorists. It may also be required to conduct humanitarian operations to deliver aid to civilians after natural disasters. In these scenarios, the landing craft, hovercrafts, and fast ribs used by amphibious forces are ideal for manoeuvring across these demanding environments. These assets can be operated from shore bases or amphibious warfare vessels off shore to conduct patrols, carrying heavily armed detachments of marines to board or inspect civilian craft.

ABOVE: Raiding missions against enemy coastal defences can help shape the battlespace, by undermining enemy morale and distracting attention. (MOD/CROWN COPYRIGHT)

BELOW: US Marine Corps and US Navy SEAL beach reconnaissance teams provide essential intelligence on the state of enemy defences and environmental conditions. (USMC)

Storming the Beach

Amphibious Landing Tactics

Marines jumping off the ramps of landing craft onto an enemy held beach is a classic image of amphibious warfare. Getting that landing craft to the shore is a far from easy task and before they are even launched towards their objective complex battle preparation is required.

Choreographing all the moving parts of an amphibious operation requires experienced and trained staff, who are able to juggle all the different elements. A clear chain of command is essential, with an overall commander assigned to execute an amphibious operation. They in turn organise their forces by task. The amphibious shipping and landing craft, as well as transport helicopters, are normally assigned to an amphibious task force, which operates off shore. Offensive air and fire support has its own commander and control staff. The ground component, often called the landing force, has its own commander and headquarters, which once ashore fight the battle to defeat the enemy's land forces.

Once amphibious commanders have received reports from their beach reconnaissance teams about environmental conditions and the deployment of enemy troops around key objectives, they are then able to develop their plan.

Hard earned experience has taught amphibious commanders that the last thing they should do is launch a direct attack on fully alerted enemy defences. Gallipoli, Dieppe, Omaha Beach, and Iwo Jima showed that troops approaching beaches in slow moving boats or landing craft were highly vulnerable.

There are ways to put troops ashore on enemy coastlines without sending them directly in to face enemy fire. Heavy and accurate fire support is a way to neutralise enemy beach defences. Helicopters now offer a way to fly over the enemy's beach defences and seize ground behind them, a tactic called 'vertical envelopment'. Helicopter-inserted marines can then fan out to destroy enemy defences to allow follow-up waves of troops to land on beaches in

safety. Deception is a key element in amphibious warfare, keeping the enemy guessing about where any landing will take place and then putting troops ashore where the enemy's defences are weakest or non-existent.

Effective fire support for amphibious landings requires complex co-ordination between fire controllers with assault troops and warships, gun batteries, or aircraft providing firepower.

Pre-programmed or scheduled fire support against land targets have long been a feature of amphibious assaults but once the landing force approaches the beach it is essential that fire controllers with the first wave of troops ashore are able to put down fire on emerging targets.

A fire support co-ordination centre in the flag ship of the amphibious force has the job of building a fire plan that brings together the fire support assets. Naval gunfire is the most readily available fire support for amphibious troops. Frigates and destroyers have large calibre guns, of a similar hitting power to 155mm field guns and they can hit targets more than 20km away. Crucially, they are fed ammunition by automated loading systems that means one gun turret on a warship can put down as much firepower, per minute, as a battery of six army field guns. The suppression effect of sustained barrages from naval

RIGHT: The landing force brings an initial wave of armoured vehicles into the bridgehead. (US DOD)

gun fire is very effective at forcing enemy troops to keep their heads down as landing craft approach the beach.

The next most effective fire support comes from strike jets, or attack helicopters, flying off aircraft carriers or warships. Highly accurate guided missiles are ideal for knocking out enemy bunkers or gun emplacements.

Controlling all this firepower requires highly trained specialists, who are qualified to direct naval gun fire and integrate air strikes. These are different skill sets and often fire control teams include enough personnel to allow different officers to simultaneously direct both types of fire support. Naval gunnery observers have to transmit co-ordinates to warships providing fire support and then once the shells start landing, they have to adjust, or correct, the fire to ensure it is on target.

Forward air controllers (FAC), or terminal joint attack controllers (JTACs), are expert at directing air strikes. The key part of their job is to ensure that the pilots of strike aircraft, or attack helicopters, have properly identified their targets. Laser designators speed up this process by bouncing a laser light off the target into the aircraft, which then uses a computer to automatically programme guided weapons with target co-ordinates. If technology is not available, then the FAC has to verbally direct the pilot to the target in a radio conversation, using key landmarks to help him identify the target.

BELOW: British Royal Marine units have Swedish made Bv206 all terrain vehicles to provide mobility in the froze Arctic North of Norway. (MOD/CROWN COPYRIGHT)

ABOVE: Amphibious forces need to be prepared to operate in all climates and environments. Britain's Royal Marines are experts are amphibious operations in the Arctic. (MOD/CROWN COPYRIGHT)

Only once the FAC is satisfied that the pilot is spot on target, will he clear the aircraft to drop weapons. The devastating impact of large aerial bombs means that these weapons have to be dropped at a safe distance from friendly troops. Although in emergency situations when friendly forces are threatened with being overrun by superior enemy troops, procedures exist for FACs to declare "danger close", to allow bombs to be dropped almost on top of friendly troops.

The pinpoint targeting of enemy coastal defences can often be enough to completely neutralise resistance and avoid assault forces being pinned down on beaches. Hence the need for fire controllers to go ashore with the first wave of assault troops so they are immediately able to start bringing fire to bear on the enemy. Back on the task force flagship, the fire support co-ordination teams have the important task of de-conflicting the naval gunfire, air support and movement of transport helicopters in the air space above the landing zone so that friendly aircraft, helicopters, ships, and ground forces are not hit by accident.

Once the enemy defences are neutralised by fire, then the landing force can be put ashore. Helicopters are increasingly used to carry out the vertical envelopment of beach defences. By flying contingents of assault troops inland, they are able to quickly identify key objects, such as high ground overlooking landing beaches, port facilities, or bridges needed to move inland.

The rapid arrival of marines by helicopter, often at night, is intended to take any enemy defenders by surprise and allow the assault force to quickly seize their objectives. They will then move to mop up any enemy troops defending the main landing beaches so the landing force can safely come ashore.

Modern heavy lift helicopters, such as the CH-53E Sea Stallion or C/MH-47 Chinook, have the capability to reach hundreds of kilometres inland thanks to their in-flight refuelling capability giving amphibious forces the potential to strike far from the sea. The MV-22B Osprey has an even longer range and more deployment options. These platforms allow the marines to exploit their success using mainly follow-on airlifted forces if it is not possible link up with sea-landed forces.

Only once the risk is judged to be at a manageable level will the landing force be launched ashore in its landing craft, hovercrafts, or landing ships. Operational planners need to manage this stage of the assault carefully. Landing ships are usually filled with hundreds of troops, dozens of vehicles, and large quantities of supplies. There is little room or time to juggle how all these men and materials will be loaded onto landing craft, or helicopters, so very detailed loading schedules need to be developed, often before amphibious vessels sail from their home ports. This means vehicles that need to be unloaded last needed to be loaded first into the vehicle deck of dock ships, so the most important vehicles can be unloaded first into landing craft as they arrive to take on cargo before heading to landing beaches.

First off, the landing ships are usually amphibious armoured assault vehicles that have the ability to 'swim' ashore. These are mostly modified armoured personnel carriers fitted with floatation equipment and propeller drives. They are the modern equivalent of the LVT armoured tractors and DD tanks from World War Two. Their job is delivering squads of marines onto the beach and moving them off the shore line, under armoured protection. Their turret mounted cannons, or machine guns, allow them to immediately bring fire to bear as they emerge from the water. Their infantry squads then have the job of mopping up any remaining pockets of resistance.

The next wave of landing craft contains the bulk of the marine infantry, and their job is to

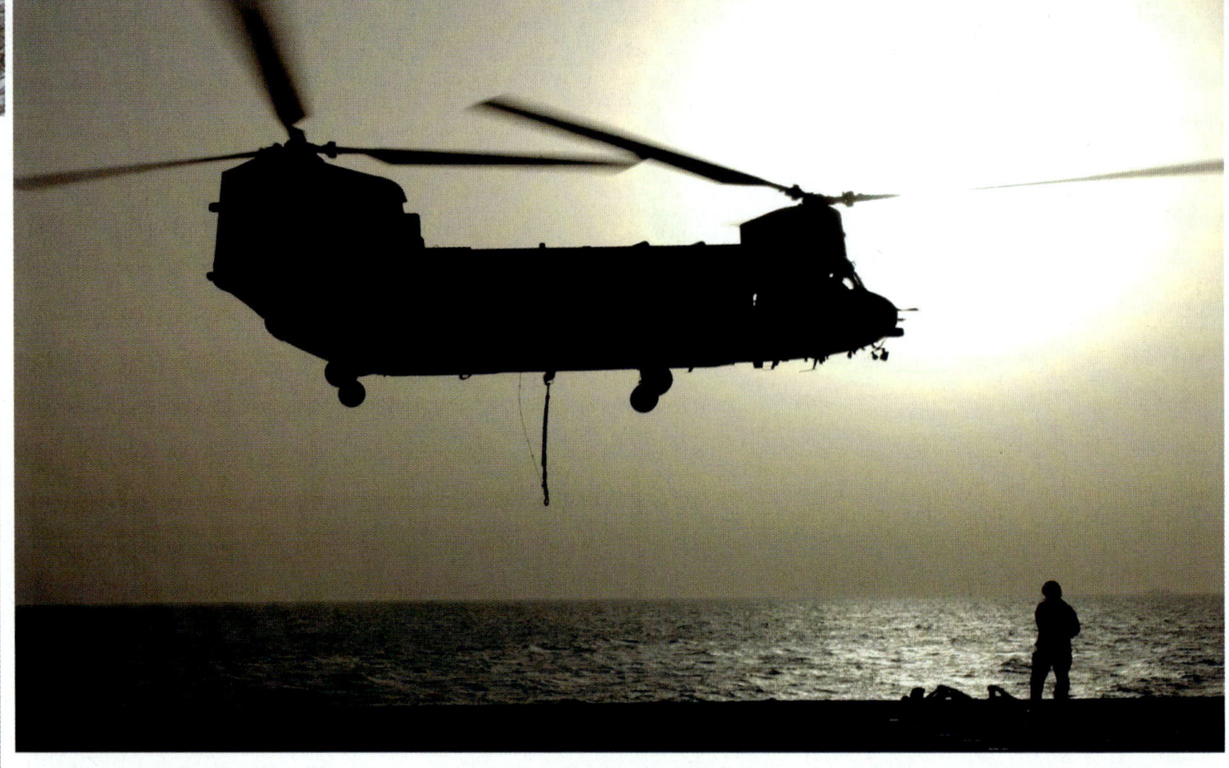

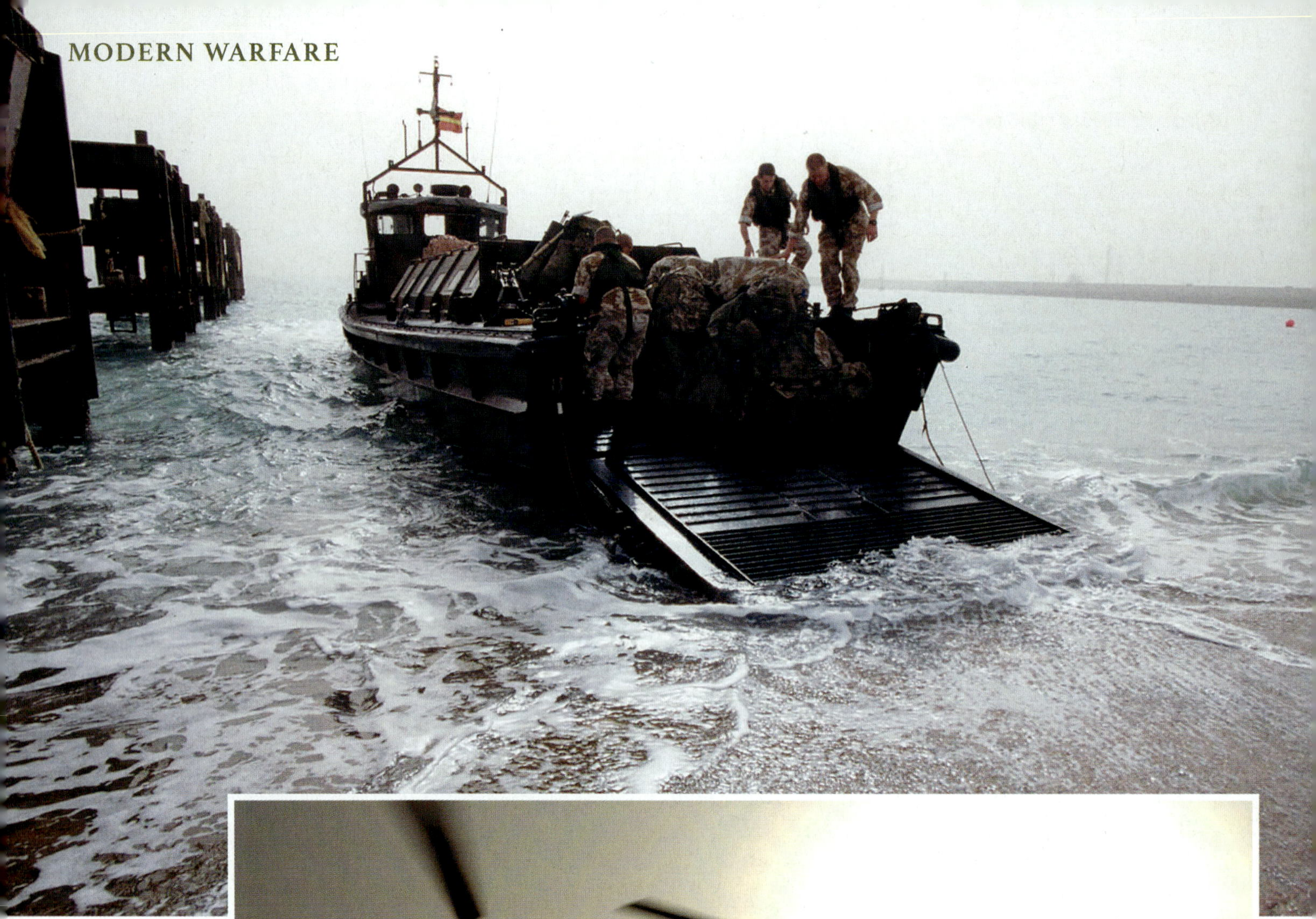

ABOVE: Landing craft have a key role bringing ashore bulk cargo to sustain a landing force ashore.
(MOD/CROWN COPYRIGHT)

RIGHT: An RAF Chinook prepares to hook up a cargo pallet from a Royal Navy warship during the 2003 Al Faw operation.
(MOD/CROWN COPYRIGHT)

secure the beachhead, setting up security positions to block enemy counterattacks. They carry ashore their wire guided anti-tank missiles, mortars and shoulder launched surface-to-air-missile (SAM) systems to build a layered defence around the beachhead. Once ashore and in position, these marines will start digging trenches and fire positions to protect them from enemy artillery fire or air strikes.

This is the time for the marine infantry to begin sending out patrols around the beachhead to establish the status of any remaining enemy forces in the vicinity and identity routes for further advances. A so-called 'active defence' prevents the enemy massing his forces for a counterattack and taking back the beachhead until its defences are fully established. Attack is the best form of defence, goes the mantra.

On the shore, the marine infantry command post will now be up and running to take over control of the beachhead and co-ordinate the arrival of follow-on forces.

This is the point when field engineers and their equipment need to move ashore to help improve the access of the beachhead. Tracked and heavy wheeled vehicles can easily turn beaches and access routes off beaches into rutted and impassable bogs. Rain and high tides can quickly make things even worse. Metal temporary roadways can be laid to negate these problems. Military police detachments have the job of controlling traffic to ensure vehicles stick to one-way systems and do not block access routes off the beach.

To avoid being contained in their beachheads, amphibious commanders are very keen to begin exploiting any successes and keeping the enemy off balance. Marine infantry units have this job and once they have gained space, follow-on units and logistic support have more room to come ashore into the beachhead.

The key to the launching of successful offensive operations is the rapid movement ashore of artillery batteries along with their ammunition. Picking the right moment to bring guns ashore requires careful judgement. If a beachhead is too small, then artillery gun lines can become vulnerable to enemy counter-battery fire because they cannot be rapidly moved to alternative fire positions. Ensuring a steady supply of ammunition is essential to ensuring guns are always ready to fire when necessary. It is sometimes more effective to have fewer guns but more ammunition ashore.

Keeping a constant flow of food, ammunition, water, and fuel ashore is the key to keeping the beachhead fighting. Bulk supplies are usually moved by landing craft, on board large trucks, They help to get huge quantities of supplies ashore quickly, but amphibious forces often operate on islands or terrain without roads and firm ground. This is where small landing craft or raiding boats come into their own, allowing supplies to be delivered to isolated detachments of marines. Helicopters can also help in the logistic effort, under-slinging pallets of cargo ➲

LEFT: Logistic support operations by helicopter need to go on around the clock, using night-vision goggles. (MOD/CROWN COPYRIGHT)

BELOW: Modern landing craft can be modified to provide shelter for troops when they operate in extreme climates. (MOD/CROWN COPYRIGHT)

or bladders of fuel or water. Flying artillery ammunition direct to gun lines is a vital job for helicopters to bypass any logistic bottlenecks on beaches and ensure that high rates of fire can be maintained.

Maintaining the health, morale, and fighting spirit of troops ashore in a beachhead is crucially dependent on the provisions of effective medical support. Surgical teams move quickly ashore to set up field hospitals or clearing centres. Their job is to receive casualties from frontline first aid posts and immediately stabilise them. Once casualties are fit to be moved, they can be transported out to the fleet for longer term treatment, either by helicopter or boat. Most large amphibious ships have hospital facilities to conduct more extensive surgery on casualties who cannot be moved out of the battle area.

The next task of engineer units is to build helicopter landing sites to allow transport and attack helicopters to move ashore from

RIGHT: Mine clearing diving teams have to get to work immediately to ensure that beachheads are free from mines and other under water obstacles.
(MOD/CROWN COPYRIGHT)

BELOW: Once ashore, the main landing force needs to rapidly position its infantry units to protect its beachhead.
(MOD/CROWN COPYRIGHT)

the fleet. This involves building metal landing pads to accommodate helicopters, as well as fuel bladder farms and ammunition dumps. The establishment of forward landing zones can also eventually allow AV-8B Harrier, or F-35B Lightning II, jump jets to come ashore.

By moving aviation assets ashore, it allows the amphibious fleet to pull further offshore to reduce their exposure to enemy air and missile attack, or to allow them to sail back to their home port to pick up reinforcements.

Once the amphibious force is firmly ashore and immediate threats to a beachhead neutralised, it is time to think about how the campaign will progress. Attention will be given to seizing an established port or major airport. This will allow follow-on army units to begin flowing into the beachhead either to take over garrison duties or take on the main enemy forces with tanks or other heavy armour. This will allow the withdrawal of the lightly equipped amphibious force to re-group, re-fit and re-set for future operations.

The key skill for amphibious commanders is managing the transfer of command from the embarked amphibious task force to the landing force as the operation progressively evolves into a land battle. So, in the approach phase the amphibious task force commander is in the lead, controlling the loading and delivering of assault units. When troops are in landing craft or helicopters, they are under naval command. Once the marines hit the beach, the marine commanders take over to control the fight against enemy troops.

As the troops and their support logistics move ashore, the balance of command switches to the landing force. Warships and aircraft offshore are now the subordinate elements, providing support to the landing force as it moves inland.

Understanding and operating according to these command procedures takes extensive training to ensure than everyone understands their place in the constantly evolving battle. For this reason, most nations have decided to keep dedicated amphibious forces in existence, even though few countries have actually carried out an amphibious operation in recent years. The corporate knowledge needed to pull off a successful amphibious landing is easily lost. Countries give it up at their peril.

ABOVE: Beach armoured recovery vehicles, or BARVs, provide an essential service to pull bogged in vehicles and vessels off beaches. The Royal Marines latest BARV, nicknamed the Hippo, entered service in 2002. It is based on a converted Leopard 1A5 tank chassis. (MOD/CROWN COPYRIGHT)

BELOW: Bulk logistic supplies, including ISO containers, need to be carried ashore on large trucks embarked on landing craft to help build stockpiles in beachheads. (MOD/CROWN COPYRIGHT)

Evacuate the Embassy!

NEOs and Humanitarian Operations

ABOVE: A US Navy LCAC hovercraft comes ashore in Indonesia after the 2005 tsunami and shows the scale of the devastation faced by US Marines dispatched to assist with the recovery effort. (MOD/CROWN COPYRIGHT)

An important role of amphibious forces are intervention missions to protect citizens and diplomats caught up in foreign conflicts or crisis. Ever since colonial times in the 18th and 19th centuries, naval vessels have landed marines on expeditions to rescue citizens in danger. The 1899 international mission to protect besieged embassies in the Chinese capital, Peking, was typical of these, seeing marines from several nations joining forces to fight off Boxer rebels.

In the 21st century, non-combatant evacuation operations, known as NEOs, are far more complex missions, often involving amphibious vessels, helicopters, airlifters, strike jets, and marines all working together.

Many nations give the mission of protecting their citizens and embassies or consulates overseas to their marines. The US Marine Corps famously provides marine security detachments at every US embassy. If an embassy comes under threat from a foreign invasion or civil unrest, the call comes out for diplomats and at-risk citizens to be evacuated.

RIGHT: US Marines land at the US Embassy in Phnom Penh in April 1975 to extract diplomats and civilians threatened by the advance of communist forces towards the Cambodian city. (US MARINE CORPS)

Amphibious ships are often pre-positioned during periods of growing tension to be ready to mount a rescue if the situation should escalate.

Once an ambassador issues a request to launch an evacuation, the rescue force will be mobilised. Helicopters are generally the quickest way to get troops to the crisis. First, they will have to fly in a security force of marines to set up a protective cordon around the embassy or at a suitable evacuation site, such as an airport.

A call will then go out for at-risk passport holders to move to the evacuation point to be processed and prepared for loading onto helicopters. A shuttle of helicopters will then take the civilians out to the waiting fleet off shore.

It may be the case that helicopters are not the best way to safely move evacuees and fixed wing aircraft could be used, if a secure airport were available. Dispatching landing craft or amphibious assault vehicles to a beachhead or a port are also NEO options.

Following natural disasters - earthquakes, tidal waves, volcanic eruptions, or hurricanes – military forces, including marines and amphibious ships are often mobilised to lead rescue and relief missions.

Many nations keep their amphibious forces at high readiness for crisis response missions, so they are well placed to be dispatched to disaster zones. The capabilities designed for amphibious assaults are ideally suited to delivering aid to locations were normal communications and transport infrastructure – harbours, airports, and bridges – have been put out of action. Landing craft and helicopters are ideal for moving around flooded terrain and dock ships can deliver large numbers of vehicles to places where there are no functioning ports.

An additional important advantage is that amphibious tasks groups, as well as their supporting landing force and aviation elements, are routinely

LEFT: Dutch Marines joined the rescue effort to help Netherlands Caribbean territories by providing communications and security patrols to prevent looting after Hurricane Irma hit in 2017. (NETHERLANDS MINISTRY OF DEFENCE)

trained to operate together so when the call comes to deploy in response to natural disasters, they can swing into action immediately. Time and again, the command-and-control capability of amphibious forces is the crucial glue that holds together demanding relief operations.

While humanitarian operations do not normally require the use of combat capabilities, it is not unknown for marines to have to undertake security patrols to maintain law and order until civilian police forces can get back up and running.

The inherent flexibility of amphibious forces mean they are often called upon to take on missions in unforeseen circumstances, at very short notice. Often the 'can do' and 'adaptable' state of mind of amphibious warriors makes the difference in situations short of all-out war.

BELOW: Royal Marines were dispatched to the Caribbean in 2017 to help British overseas territories recover from the impact of Hurricane Irma. Here Mexeflote is employed by the Royal Logistics Corps to bring ashore a contingent of Royal Marines on the island of Anguilla. (MOD/CROWN COPYRIGHT)

Amphibious Warriors

Marines of the World

RIGHT: Marines from all around the world have a reputation for being elite troops and they undergo demanding training regimes to prepare them for the conditions experienced in amphibious operations.
(US NAVY)

BELOW: Storming the beach. Beach assaults during training exercises can look very dramatic. Operating from ships and helicopters requires marine units to be trained to a high standard.
(EVGEN SYLKIN, UKRAINE, MINISTRY OF DEFENCE)

Marines are often called 'sea soldiers' and they are recognised as elite troops, who are highly trained for combat both on sea and land. The term is derived from the ancient Latin word marinus which loosely translated means 'of the sea'.

The Greeks, Romans and Vikings all had warriors who were trained and equipped to serve in their fleets and then invade enemy territory. When European nations sent fleets sailing on the wars of colonial conquest in the 16th and 17th centuries, they formed special units of soldiers to serve in their fleets. The first job was to maintain discipline among ship's crews and then to send landing parties ashore to claim territory. These were the first northern European units to be known as marines.

In the 20th century, many nations transformed their marine units into specialist amphibious forces to carry out raids on enemy territory or capture bridgeheads on enemy coasts. They were put through intensive training to fight in small groups, with minimal fire and logistic support. This included close quarter combat, the operation of landing craft and beach assault tactics.

Modern amphibious warriors are often called marines, but several nations call them naval infantry or coastal troops. Some nations have small armed forces, with dual role army regiments with an amphibious role.

No matter, amphibious warriors from around the world are noted for their unique esprit de corps and fighting skills. The US Marine Corps, Britain's Royal Marines and Russia's Naval Infantry have long traditions of success in battle that means they set the standard for today's amphibious warriors.

Algeria's amphibious forces are a relatively new development, with the North African country's first Marine Fusiliers battalions only being formed in 1986, as part of the Algerian Naval Forces.

In 2005, the amphibious branch was expanded with the formation of the Marine Commandos Corps.

Algeria armed forces are well equipped and well resourced thanks to the country's oil and gas wealth. Since the country's independence from France in 1962, Algeria's military have been focused on defeating Islamic insurgents but, in recent years, tension with Morocco and Western Sahara has prompted efforts to bolster its conventional combat capabilities against external threats.

The build-up of amphibious forces began in the 1980s, following the purchase of two landing ships from Britain in 1984 and additional units were formed after the delivery of a larger amphibious dock ship in 2015.

The Marine Fusiliers, like the Parachute Commandos of the Algerian Land Forces, are recognised as elite units of the Algerian military and they undergo intensive training for their role.

Under Algerian military doctrine, airborne and amphibious forces are intended to strike deep into an opponent's rear areas.

The Marine Fusilier units are also a rapid-action and special operations force. They are fully autonomous and have their own logistics, combat, and support capabilities to allow them

Algeria

Marine Commando Corps

to rapidly mobilise against internal threats to stability.

Each regiment has three fighting companies, as well as a logistics company, an anti-tank company, a surveillance company, and a transport company.

Although Algeria remains proudly independent and non-aligned, its Marine Fusilier units have participated in training exercises with the US Marine Corps, US Army, Italy's San Marco Regiment, and Spain's Marine Infantry Brigade.

ABOVE: Joint exercises with the US Marine Corps have improved the combat readiness of Algeria's marines. (US DOD)

ALGERIAN MARINE COMMANDO CORPS
(With location of home garrison)

- Navy Special Action Regiment
- 1st Marine Fusiliers Regiment 'Martyr Housh Mohamed' (Jijel)
- 3rd Marine Fusiliers Regiment (Azzefoun)
- 4th Marine Fusiliers Regiment of (El Milia)
- 5th Marine Fusiliers Regiment (Ténès)
- 7th Marine Fusiliers Regiment (Boumerdes)
- Marine Fusiliers Regiment (Dellys)
- Marine Fusiliers Regiment (Mers-El-Kebir)
- 12th Coastal Artillery Regiment 'Martyr Ferendi Mohamed' (Collo)

LEFT: Algerian marines practice boarding tactics from a Mi-17 assault helicopter. (JAWI3)

Argentina

Argentine Marine Corps

ABOVE: US and Argentine Marines carry out joint training during a UNITAS amphibious assault exercise. (US DOD)

Argentina's marines trace their history back to Spanish marines of the colonial era and then to the country's war on independence between 1810 and 1918.

In modern times the Argentine marines have been a professional unit under the command of the country's navy. They played a leading role in the 1982 conflict with Britain over the Falkland Islands, or Malvinas as they are known to the Argentines. Marines were the first amphibious units to land at Port Stanley in Operation Rosario during the early hours of April 2, 1982.

Twenty LVTP-7AI tracked amphibious armoured personnel carriers led the assault by 550 Argentine marines which quickly overwhelmed the 77 British Royal Marines and Royal Navy sailors stationed at Port Stanley. One Argentine marine was killed and six wounded before the outnumbered and outgunned British surrendered.

The Argentine 5th Marine Battalion dug-in on Mount Tumbledown to defend the western approaches to Port Stanley. It fought a tough battle against the Scots Guards during the final British assault on the capital of the islands.

Since the Falklands war, the Argentine marines have taken part in several United Nations peacekeeping missions, including in Cyprus, Croatia, Kosovo, Haiti, and Western Sahara. Marine boarding teams were dispatched to the Middle East in 1990 onboard Argentine navy ships taking part in the UN-sanctioned embargo of Iraq.

RIGHT: The invasion of the Falklands in 1982 is the most famous recent operation of Argentina's marines. (SOMOS MAGAZINE)

ARGENTINE MARINE CORPS

Fleet Marine Force

- 2nd Marine Corps Battalion
- 3rd Marine Corps Battalion
- 1st Amphibious Vehicles Battalion
- Amphibious Engineers Battalion
- Command and Logistical Support Battalion
- 1st Communications Battalion
- 1st Field Artillery Battalion
- Anti-aircraft artillery Battalion
- Amphibious Commandos Group (APCA)

Southern Marine Force

- 4th Marine Corps Battalion
- 5th Marine Corps Battalion

Australia

Australian Army

Australia has never had an independent marine force but has chosen to train up units of its army into the amphibious role. The World War One landings at Gallipoli are perhaps Australia's most famous amphibious operations, even through the landings proved a failure. In World War Two, Australian troops joined the US in the island-hopping campaign against the Japanese in the Pacific.

In 2011, the Australian Defence Force (ADF) launched a new initiative to establish an Amphibious Ready Group, or ARG. New amphibious shipping was ordered and the 2nd Battalion, Royal Australian Regiment (2 RAR), based at Lavarack Barracks, in Townsville, became an amphibious light infantry battalion.

The battalion's primary role is to provide specialist capabilities to conduct what are termed pre-landing activities. It includes small boat operators and reconnaissance and sniper teams as well as command, communications, and logistics elements. The battalion has a strength of around 350 personnel.

A new structure was announced in January 2018 which comprised a battalion headquarters, a security company with four infantry platoons, a support company, and an administration company. It is supported by electronic warfare teams, amphibious beach teams, Royal Australian Navy clearance divers and other specialist elements.

The role of the pre-landing battalion is to be first ashore in any amphibious operation and then to secure the initial bridgehead. This will allow follow on forces from the ARG's Ground Combat Element (GCE), which is based on another army infantry battalion, to come ashore. Different units rotate through the role on an annual basis.

LEFT: Soldiers of the 2nd Battalion, Royal Australian Regiment helocast from an MRH-90 during an amphibious exercise off the eastern coast of Australia. (USMC)

BELOW: The 2nd Battalion, Royal Australian Regiment, is Australia's specialist pre-landing unit, which has the mission of being first ashore during amphibious operations. (US NAVY)

China

People's Liberation Army Navy Marine Corps

RIGHT: A Chinese sailor with a boarding team assigned to the guided missile destroyer PLANS *Haikou* climbs a ladder to board the national security cutter USCGC *Waesche* during a 2014 maritime security exercise in the Pacific Ocean. (US DOD)

China has been building up its amphibious landing forces over the past two decades as part of its military modernisation effort. The focus of this drive is to give Beijing the option of staging an amphibious assault to seize Taiwan or other islands in the South China Sea.

The People's Liberation Army Navy Marine Corps (PLANMC) is one of five major branches of the PLA Navy (PLAN). It is trained and equipped for amphibious warfare, expeditionary operations, and rapid responses.

Over the past 70 years the PLANMC has gone through several re-organisations. It was first formed in April 1953 with the intention of launching a major amphibious assault to capture Taiwan. This coincided with the Korean war, when Chinese communist troops where directly involved in combat with US forces. Eight PLANMC divisions were formed, and the force grew quickly to 110,000 troops.

The corps was disbanded in 1957 as part of a shake up in the Chinese military's high command but several naval infantry regiments, organised along Soviet lines, were retained to support the PLAN fleet coastal defence operations.

In 1979, the PLANMC was reformed, and a renewed effort was launched to develop an amphibious landing capability. The 1st Marine Brigade was activated on Hainan to begin experimenting with amphibious assault tactics.

Subsequently, several People's Liberation Army (PLA) Ground Force units were transferred to PLANMC to be converted into amphibious brigades. These included the 164th Motorized Infantry Division, which became the Zhanjiang-based 164th Marine Brigade.

BELOW: The Type 05 is an amphibious tracked armoured fighting vehicles developed by Norinco for the People's Liberation Army Navy Marine Corp. (RUSSIAN MINISTRY OF DEFENCE)

PEOPLE'S LIBERATION ARMY NAVY MARINE CORPS

South Sea Fleet
- 1st Marine Brigades (Zhanjiang)
- 2nd (ex-164th) Marine Brigades (Zhanjiang)
- 4th Marine Brigade (Jieyang)

East Sea Fleet
- 3rd Marine Brigade (Jinjiang)

North Sea Fleet
- 5th Marine Brigade (Laoshan)
- 6th Marine Brigade based (Haiyang)

Centrally Controlled Units
- Aviation Brigade
- Chemical Defence Brigade
- Artillery Brigade
- Engineering Brigade
- Jiaolong Commando Brigade (Hainan)

The modern PLANMC comprises 40,000 personnel, grouped into seven amphibious brigades and four specialist support brigades, including aviation, chemical defence, artillery, and combat engineering. The combined arms brigades have 6,000 personnel and each include three marine or manoeuvre battalions, equipped with the ZTD-05 Amphibious Tank, ZBD-05 Amphibious fighting vehicles, and VP4 amphibious tracked vehicles. They also have air assault, artillery, air defence, reconnaissance, and logistic battalions.

The Jiaolong special operations brigade has a raiding role and has deployed on overseas maritime security missions.

The PLANMC units are distributed between the PLAN's three naval commands, with 18,000 marines deployed with the South Sea Fleet, 6,000 marines are assigned to the East Sea Fleet and 12,000 assigned to the North Sea Fleet.

The PLANMC's roles include non-war military activities (NWMA) to support and protect China's overseas trade interests including resources, infrastructure, and citizens abroad.

Although operations in the South China Sea region are the focus of current PLANMC activity, the corps maintains a presence at China's first overseas military base in Djibouti on the Red Sea coast of Africa. This extends Chinese military reach and strategic influence in Africa and the Middle East. A contingent of marines are also routinely embarked on PLAN warships sailing in the Gulf of Aden as part of a counterpiracy-mission that supports China's trade interests in the region. The PLANMC detachment in Djibouti supports China's military engagement objectives, by conducting joint training with Thai, Pakistani, Saudi, South African, and Djiboutian forces.

The PLANMC has traditionally focused on assaulting and defending small reef and island outposts across the South China Sea but more recently it has expanded its ambitions to include complex expeditionary operations.

Recent exercises have included complex all-arms training, combining amphibious, air, naval and fire support operations. The PLANMC aviation brigade has been conducting three-dimensional amphibious assault training which included air assault components, amphibious assault vehicles, and a combination of Landing CraftAir Cushion (LCAC), or hovercraft, and assault boats.

During these exercises PLANMC assault units seize initial bridgeheads and then a follow-up wave of PLA Ground Force units is landed from commercial roll-on/roll-off vessels so they can move inland to engage the enemy's main land forces.

ABOVE: Chinese marines have a maritime security role in counter-piracy missions in the Indian Ocean. (US NAVY)

BELOW: A decade ago, relations between China and the United States were cordial and joint training exercises, including involving the PLAN Marine Corps, were regularly held. (US NAVY)

Brazil

Naval Fusilier Corps

ABOVE: Brazilian Marine Corps Special Operations Battalion operators carry out a joint training exercise with US Navy SEALs. (US NAVY)

As the largest and most populous South American nation, Brazil has the continent's largest armed forces and navy. Its Naval Fusilier Corps is currently 15,000 strong and is an all-professional force.

The corps traces its origins back to 1808 when the troops of the Portuguese Royal Brigade of the Navy arrived in Brazil during the colonial era, when Queen Mary I and her son Prince Regent, DomJoão, relocated to the then Portuguese South American territory.

In retaliation for the invasion of Portugal by Napolean's troops, Dom João ordered the invasion of French Guiana, and the Portuguese marines were heavily involved in this campaign.

After Brazilian independence in 1825, the marine force received many names and underwent various reorganisations. It was involved in several wars and campaigns, including the War of the Independence of Brazil, conflicts in the River Plate basin, and the Paraguayan War.

In the modern era, the Brazilian marines have an amphibious landing force, known as the Fleet Marine Force, which is configured for conventional war fighting as well as several small regional units. These are trained and equipped for riverine operations in the Amazon and Pantanal regions. Marine units also provide security for naval bases and overseas embassies.

Brazilian marine units have participated in the United Nations peacekeeping and humanitarian operations in Bosnia, Honduras, Mozambique, Rwanda, Angola, East Timor, and Haiti.

NAVAL FUSILIER CORPS

Fleet Marine Force

- Command and Control Battalion

- 1st 'Riachuelo' Marine Infantry Battalion

- 2nd 'Humaitá' Marine Infantry Battalion

- 3rd 'Paissandu' Marine Infantry Battalion

- Marine Artillery Battalion

- Marine Armoured Vehicle Battalion

- Marine Tactical Air Control and Air Defence Battalion

Reinforcement Troops

- Marine Engineer Battalion

- Marine Logistic Battalion

- Amphibious Vehicles Battalion

- Police Company

- Landing Support Company

Marine Special Operations Battalion 'Tonelero'

RIGHT: Boarding operations are the job of the Brazilian Marine Corps Special Operations Battalion. (US NAVY)

Chile

Marine Infantry Corps

LEFT: US and Chilean Marines train near Valparaiso, Chile, ahead of a United Nations deployment to Haiti. (US DOD)

BELOW: A boarding exercise by Chilean marines helps build the country's marine security capability. (US NAVY)

Chile's modern marines have their origins in the forces formed to fight Spanish rule during the country's war of independence. The leader of the independence forces, Don Bernardo O'Higgins Riquelme, formally established his first marine unit in June 1818. However, revolutionary naval units formed at the start of the war in 1812 had their own marine detachment, known as Cazadores de los Andes, of 25 sea soldiers aboard the warship *Aguila*.

O'Higgins's decree described the role of his marines, saying: "these people will fire rifles from the deck, [and] will handle the machete in boardings and bayonet and cannon in landings."

Today, the Chilean Marine Infantry Corps has the mission of helping project naval power, "to safeguard sovereignty and territorial integrity and to promote and defend national interests abroad."

As well as combat operations in times of war, the 5,500 strong corps also have to be ready for humanitarian operations, disaster support, support for public order, stabilisation, and international cooperation.

The Expeditionary Amphibious Brigade forms the amphibious component of the corps, and it is trained and equipped to operate in any terrain, from the desert regions of the country's north to the near Arctic conditions in the far south. Two marine detachments, equipped with artillery and coastal defence missiles, form the Protection Force. The corps also provide Naval Detachments of Order and Security to protect naval bases.

Chilean marines have served in United Nations peacekeeping missions in Cyprus and Haiti. They also participate in the joint Chilean-Argentine Peace Force, which supports UN missions around the world.

CHILEAN MARINE INFANTRY CORPS

Expeditionary Amphibious Brigade

- Headquarters Company
- 21st Marine Battalion 'Miller'
- 31st Marine Battalion 'Aldea'
- 41st Marine Combat Support Battalion 'Hurtado'
- 51st Marine Logistic Battalion

Protection Forces

- 1st Marine Detachment 'Lynch' (Fort Condell)
- 4th Marine Detachment 'Cochrane' (Río de losCiervos)

Egypt

Egyptian Amphibious Brigades

RIGHT: The Egyptian army provides the landing elements for the country's amphibious force, including T-55 and T-55 tanks, as well as other armoured vehicles. (US DOD)

EGYPTIAN AMPHIBIOUS FORCES

111th Independent Mechanized Brigade

- 42nd Mechanized Infantry Battalion
- 43rd Mechanized Infantry Battalion
- 44th Mechanized Infantry Battalion

153rd Naval Commandos Group

- 515th Naval Commandos Battalion
- 616th Naval Commandos Battalion
- 818th Naval Commandos Battalion

BELOW: An Egyptian OT-62B armoured personnel carrier comes ashore from a utility landing craft during an amphibious assault in support of the Bright Star '85 multi-national amphibious exercise. (US DOD)

Egypt's armed forces have a long tradition of amphibious operations stretching back to ancient times when the fleets of the Pharaohs built empires around the Mediterranean and Red Sea regions.

During the 19th and early 20th centuries Britain dominated Egypt and its armed forces were directed by colonial authorities. Egyptian marines were formed during the 1860s along the lines of the British Royal Marines Light Infantry and they served in several colonial period expeditions. A joint force of British and Egyptian marines also served in Greece during World War One.

During the 1960s and 1970s, Soviet influence grew in Egypt after the failed Anglo-French intervention to seize the Suez Canal in 1956. In 1972 as part of Egypt's preparations to launch an offensive across the Suez canal, the Soviets helped set up a brigade-sized amphibious force.

The 130th Amphibious Brigade was equipped with Soviet-built PT-76 and BTR-50 amphibious armoured vehicles and it played an important role in the 1973 Yom Kippur War. It spearheaded the Egyptian offensive by launching an amphibious assault across the Great Bitter Lake to take Israeli defences by surprise and then moved toward the Mitla and Gidi passes.

After Egypt signed a peace treaty with Israel in 1979, the country began to receive military aid from the United States. The 130th Brigade then started to participate in the annual series of Bright Star amphibious exercises with US Marine Corps units.

This 130th brigade was originally formed as part of the Egyptian army and it has since been re-named as the 111th Independent Mechanized Brigade, which has a strength of around 1,500 soldiers. The Egyptian army's 153rd Naval Commandos Group is also trained as a special forces raiding unit, focused on maritime environments.

France

9th Marine Infantry Brigade

France's marines have a long and distinguished history, stretching back to 1622 when the famous Cardinal Richelieu ordered the formation of sea companies of soldiers to serve on navy ships. These companies were used to embark on warships to serve guns and participate in the boarding of enemy ships.

The Troupes de Marine was formed to spearhead the expansion of France's empire in Africa and the Far East during the 19th century. In the 20th century, France's marine infantry fought in the bloody campaigns to preserve the country's empires in Indo-China and Algeria.

With the ending of French rule in Algeria in 1962, the marine infantry regiments returned to metropolitan France to become the core of the country's new intervention or rapid reaction force. The successor to this unit is now the 9th Marine Infantry Brigade of the French Army. It is trained and equipped to carry out amphibious assault operations.

The main units of the brigade are equipped with light armoured vehicles and light artillery, so it can also operate as a manoeuvre force in conventional and counter-insurgency operations.

The brigade is France's contribution to the Anglo-French rapid reaction force set up in 2010. The nation's marine infantry units have always been manned by professional soldiers and during the 1990s they were routinely deployed on United Nations and NATO peacekeeping missions in Bosnia, Kosovo, and Afghanistan.

Several units from the brigade also deployed to Mali from 2013 on the French-led campaign against Islamic insurgents in the north African country.

Free French Commando units were trained in amphibious raiding by the British during World War Two, and their successors are now the French navy's special forces raiding units. French Navy marine fusilier or rifle units guard French naval bases.

LEFT: Marine Infantrymen from the 1er RIMa practice urban combat tactics. (ARMÉE DE TERRE)

BELOW: In February 2022, elements of the 3rd Marine Infantry Regiment, the 11th RAMa and the 6th Engineer Regiment embarked on the FS *Mistral* for the Mission Jeanne d'Arc amphibious deployment to the Indian Ocean. (ARMÉE DE TERRE)

Italy

San Marco Marine Brigade

As ancient maritime powers, Italy's city states had a long tradition of embarking sea soldiers on naval vessels as they battled for supremacy and protection of their trade around the Mediterranean. The Republic of Venice formed its first marine unit in 1550. The modern Italian state emerged from the country's first war of independence in 1848 and adopted the old Kingdom of Sardina's marine infantry regiment as its first amphibious unit.

The Italian Royal Navy's Naval Infantry Brigade adopted the name San Marco during World War One because of its links to the Venice region and the name has since been associated with the Italian amphibious units.

In the 1960s, the unit was re-activated as a dedicated amphibious unit, and it was built up to support NATO amphibious forces during the Cold War period.

The modern Italian navy's amphibious force is 3,800 strong and is designated as the San Marco Marine Brigade. It contains a landing force regiment, a regiment specialising in maritime security and ship boarding, as well as naval base security regiment. The brigade is also responsible for the operation of landing craft and amphibious training across the Italian armed forces.

The San Marco Marine Brigade is part of the Italian Armed Forces' Sea Projection Force, together with the navy's Third Division, which operates amphibious shipping and the army's Cavalry Brigade 'Pozzuolo del Friuli'. This latter brigade is intended to be the follow-on land component in any major amphibious operation. It includes the Italian army's amphibious force, the 1st Lagunari Battalion.

SAN MARCO MARINE BRIGADE (BRINDISI)

- Amphibious Integration Centre
- Navy Landing Craft Group
- 1st San Marco Regiment - landing force
- 2nd San Marco Regiment - boarding operations
- 3rd San Marco Regiment - naval base security
- 1st Honor Guard Company (Rome)
- National Emergencies Company (Taranto)
- Operational Raider Group

1st Lagunari Battalion (Malcontenta)

- Manoeuvre Support Company (Mestre)
- Amphibious Reconnaissance Company (Mestre)
- Amphibious Tactical Support Company (Vignole Island)
- Training Company (Mestre)

Japan

Amphibious Rapid Deployment Brigade

The Imperial Japanese Naval Landing Forces were first formed in 1876 and played an important part in expanding Japan's empire in the run up to World War Two.

When the Japanese launched their all out offensive across the Pacific and southeast Asia after the surprise attack on the US Pacific Fleet at Pearl Harbor on December 7, 1941, the landing forces staged several amphibious operations.

Along with the rest of the Imperial military, the landing forces were disbanded by the Americans after Japan's surrender in 1945. In 1947, the

AMPHIBIOUS RAPID DEPLOYMENT BRIGADE

- 1st Amphibious Rapid Deployment Regiment
- 2nd Amphibious Rapid Deployment Regiment
- 3rd Amphibious Rapid Deployment Regiment (being formed)
- Artillery Battalion
- Reconnaissance Battalion
- Engineer Battalion
- Combat Landing Battalion
- Logistic Support Battalion

newly democratic Japan adopted a new constitution, which explicitly disavowed war as an instrument of state policy and promised that Japan would never maintain a military.

However, in response to rising Cold War tension with Red China and the Soviet Union, the Americans pushed Japan to re-interpret its constitution and form its new armed forces, which were re-branded as the Japan Self-Defense Forces (JSDF). They included, air, ground, and maritime self-defence forces, as its main components. As amphibious forces were deemed to be 'offensive',

for many decades the JSDF did without them.

During the 21st century rising tension with China prompted the Japanese government to reconsider this situation. The point of contention was the Senkaku Islands, at the southwestern end of the Ryukyu Islands chain. Their position, some 70km from the disputed island of Taiwan led to China claiming sovereignty over them.

In 2006, the Japanese government published a new defence plan that called for the eventual establishment of an amphibious force that could ➡

ABOVE: Members of the Japanese Amphibious Rapid Deployment Brigade come ashore from a LCAC during an amphibious exercise. (RIKUJOJIEITAI BOUEISHO)

BELOW: The activation ceremony for the Japanese Amphibious Rapid Deployment Brigade. (US DOD)

reinforce or re-capture the Senkaku Islands. New amphibious shipping, assault vehicles, helicopters and other specialist equipment were ordered. A dedicated landing force was eventually set up by converting a unit of the Ground Self-Defense Force (GSDF). The Western Area Infantry Regiment (WAIR) based at Camp Ainoura, near Sasebo naval base, was designed to begin amphibious training and personnel were sent to America to begin training in amphibious warfare skills with the US Marine Corps. The regiment also took part in several exercises with USMC units based in Japan.

On April 7, 2018, the Amphibious Rapid Deployment Brigade (ARDB) was formally stood up at Camp Ainoura, in Sasebo, by expanding the WAIR. It was given the task of preventing invaders from occupying Japanese islands along the edge of the East China Sea that were considered vulnerable to attack.

Since its formation, the ARDB has been steadily increasing its readiness and has conducted regular joint training with USMC units. It has also sent detachments to train in the Philippines and Australia, often in joint exercises with US forces. In 2021, the first two women soldiers began training to serve in the ARDB.

Expansion plans for the ARDB include the establishment of a third regiment and an aviation element at Kyushu on the island of Okinawa from 2025. The aviation element is to eventually consist of 17 Boeing V-22 Osprey tilt rotor aircraft, as well as around 50 Sikorsky UH060 Black Hawk transport and Boeing AH-64 Apache Longbow attack helicopters.

ABOVE: Japanese Ground Self-Defense Force troops take part in joint training during a patrolling exercise at the US Marine Corps Base Camp Pendleton, California in 2013. (US DOD)

RIGHT: Soldiers from the JGSDF Amphibious Rapid Deployment Brigade (ARDB) load equipment inside an AAV-P7/A1 assault amphibious vehicle as they prepare to depart the amphibious dock landing ship USS *Ashland*. (USNI)

Netherlands

Royal Netherlands Marine Corps

The Royal Netherlands Marine Corps is the elite naval infantry corps of the Royal Netherlands Navy. It is one of world's oldest marine units, which was originally formed in December 1665 as the Regiment de Marine by the then grand pensionary of the Dutch Republic, Johan de Witt, and his famous admiral, Michiel de Ruyter.

The corps played an important role in the establishment of the Dutch Empire in the Far East, and it helped defend the city of Rotterdam against German invaders in 1940. It was re-built with American help in World War Two as part of the build up of forces for the Pacific campaign. It did not see action but was dispatched to the Dutch East Indies to re-establish Dutch control after the surrender of Japanese occupation forces in 1945.

When the Netherlands joined NATO in 1949 it took on a role within the alliance to defend western Europe.

Since 1972, units of the Netherlands Marine Corps have formed part of the United Kingdom/Netherlands Amphibious Force (UK/NL AF), with the British 3 Commando Brigade. Consequently, Dutch marine elements are deployed annually to Norway for arctic warfare training exercises with their British counterparts.

In the 1970s, the corps was designated as the Netherland's specialist counterterrorist unit and in 1977 executed a complex hostage rescue operation to free captives held on a train. This role continues to this day via the Netherlands Maritime Special Operations Forces (NLMARSOF).

After 1990, Dutch marine units took part in United Nations and NATO peacekeeping operations in Iraq, Cambodia, Bosnia, Kosovo, Liberia, and Afghanistan. The corps currently has a strength of just over 3,000 personnel.

ABOVE: The Royal Netherlands Marine Corps are one of Europe's best trained and equipped amphibious forces. (MINISTERIE VAN DEFENSIE)

BELOW: The Netherlands Maritime Special Operations Forces (MARSOF) regularly deploy on dangerous overseas intervention missions, including leading the Netherlands mission into southern Afghanistan from 2006 to 2014. (MINISTERIE VAN DEFENSIE)

ROYAL NETHERLANDS MARINE CORPS, 2023

Headquarters Marine Corps (Van Ghent Barracks, Rotterdam)

- 1st Marine Combat Group (Van Braam Houckgeest Barracks, Doorn)
- 2nd Marine Combat Group (Van Braam Houckgeest Barracks, Doorn)
- Seabased Support Group (SSG) (Van Braam Houckgeest Barracks, Doorn)
- Surface Assault and Training Group (Joost Dourlein barracks, Texel)
- 32nd Raiding Squadron (Savaneta Barracks, Aruba, Netherlands Antilles)

Netherlands Maritime Special Operations Forces (NLMARSOF)

(Van Braam Houckgeest Barracks, Doorn, and Den Helder)

- Maritime Counter Terrorism Squadron (M-Squadron)
- Conventional Squadron (C-Squadron)
- Training Squadron (T-Squadron)
- Logistic Support Group (LSG)

Russia

Russian Naval Infantry

ABOVE: Russian naval infantry conducts regular exercises with foreign counterparts, including Indian troops. Those shown here were participating in Exercise Indra-2017 in the Primorsky region of Russia.
(RUSSIAN MINISTRY OF DEFENCE)

Russia's sea soldiers are known as Naval Infantry, and they can trace their history back to 1705 when Tsar Peter the Great formed units of soldiers to serve with his Baltic Fleet.

Tsarist naval infantry units were some of the first units to switch sides during the Revolution in 1917 and so were heralded as heroes by the Soviets. During World War Two, the naval infantry units of the Black Sea and Baltic Fleets won many battle honours for staging amphibious landings in the face of fanatical German resistance.

Since the demise of the Soviet Union in 1991, the Russian Navy has retained the Naval Infantry as a key component of its Coastal Forces. Its mission is to protect Russian's coastal regions and project power around the world. Each Russian fleet – Northern, Baltic, Black Sea, Caspian, and Pacific – has a Coastal Forces corps, which in turn contains at least one naval infantry brigade, as well as a brigade of amphibious ships.

The naval infantry brigades contain a combined arms force of infantry equipped with armoured personnel carriers (APC), tanks, self-propelled artillery, air defence, reconnaissance, medical and logistic support elements. At least one battalion from each naval infantry brigade is comprised of contract or professional soldiers and the remainder are conscripts serving only for a year in uniform. These brigades are trained and equipped to carry out amphibious landings, so their BTR-80 APCs are modified to swim ashore from landing ships.

Each fleet assigns its naval infantry specialist roles to meet their unique

RIGHT: Naval infantry brigades are the elite force of the Russian navy.
(US NAVY)

operational requirements. A major role of the 61st Naval Infantry Brigade is to project Russian power across the Arctic region. Each summer an amphibious flotilla and an embarked battalion of the 61st Brigade conducts a cruise into the Arctic to carry out landing exercises on isolated islands.

The Black Sea Fleet's 810th Naval Infantry Brigade is based in Sevastopol and manned predominately by professional personnel. This brigade played a key role in the seizure of the Crimea in 2014, when its soldiers were dubbed 'Little Green Men'. It also took part in protecting Russian air force units as they built an airbase in Syria in the summer of 2015.

The 810th Brigade played an important role in the Russian invasion of Ukraine in February 2022 and suffered heavy losses during the battle of Mariupol. The Pacific Fleet's 155th Naval Infantry Brigade took part in the attack on the Ukrainian capital Kyiv from Belarus.

After Russian forces switched the focus of their campaign to defending territory captured in southern Ukraine, all the naval infantry brigades have taken their turn to undertake tours of duty in the operational zone. This has seen them concentrate on conventional land combat and there has been a noticeable drop in amphibious training exercises across the Russian Navy's fleets.

LEFT: Soviet-era equipment, including PT-76 amphibious tanks, have now been retired and the Russian Naval Infantry has been re-equipped in recent years. (US DOD)

BELOW: Black bereted Russian naval infantrymen provide security on Russian amphibious vessels delivering supplies to Moscow's garrison in Syria.

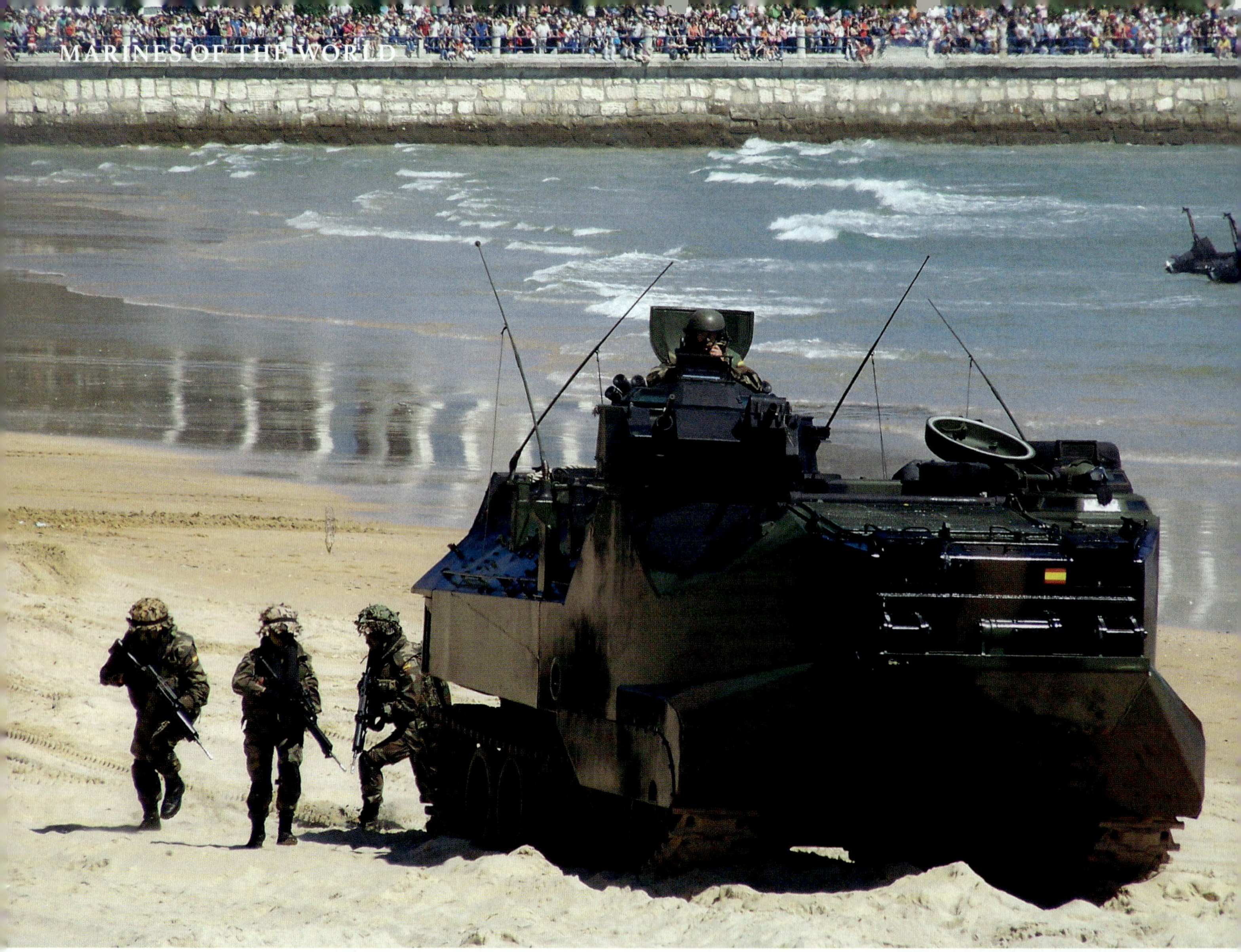

Spain

Spanish Marine Corps

ABOVE: Spanish marines operate AAV-7 armoured amphibious vehicles to deliver landing forces ashore. (STOJAKOVIC81)

RIGHT: Spanish Special Naval Warfare operatives conduct a visit, board, search, and seizure operation training exercise on a US Navy supply ship. (US DOD)

The Infantería de Armada, or Navy Infantry, was created by Charles V in 1537, making Spain's marines the world's oldest known amphibious unit. The modern Spanish Marine Corps comprises three main elements, the 'Tercio de Armada' Marine Infantry Brigade, together with the Protection Force which is responsible for security of naval bases, and the Special Naval Warfare Force.

The 3,500-strong 'Tercio de Armada' brigade is the Spanish Navy's amphibious expeditionary component, and it is tasked with power projection missions, operations in coastal waters and ground combat. It is based in San Fernando, a city to which the Marine Infantry has been linked since 1769. Since 1794, the Marine Infantry units located in San Fernando have been housed in the San Carlos Marine Battalion Barracks, which continues to be the brigade's home today. It is close to Rota Naval Base, where the amphibious ships used by the brigade are located, and it is also near to the Sierra del Retín exercise area.

MARINE INFANTRY BRIGADE 'TERCIO DE ARMADA'
• Headquarters Battalion
• 1st Landing Battalion
• 2nd Landing Battalion
• 3rd Mechanized Landing Battalion
• Amphibious Mobility Group
• Artillery Landing Group
• Combat Service Support Group

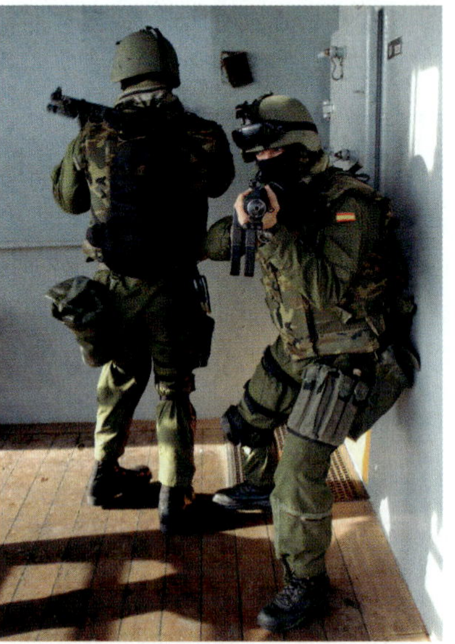

In 1975, the brigade embarked on the amphibious ships and landed in the Western Sahara to evacuate Spanish citizens from the disputed territory.

Since 1996, Spanish marines have deployed to Bosnia and Herzegovina, Haiti, Lebanon, and Afghanistan, participated in Operation Sophia in Libyan waters, Operation Atalanta against piracy in Somalia, and the European Union operation in Mali.

South Korea

Republic of Korea Marine Corps

The Republic of Korea Marine Corps (ROKMC) was founded at Deoksan airfield in Jinhae in April 1949 as part of a drive by the United States to build South Korea's armed forces. It initially had a strength of just 380 men and was equipped with mainly second-hand weapons abandoned by the Imperial Japanese Army.

REPUBLIC OF KOREA MARINE CORPS

1st Marine Division (Sea-Dragon)

- Quick Manoeuvre Force
- 2nd Marine Brigade
- 3rd Marine Brigade
- 7th Marine Brigade
- 1st Marine Artillery Brigade

2nd Marine Division (Blue-Dragon)

- 1st Marine Brigade
- 5th Marine Brigade
- 8th Marine Brigade
- 2nd Marine Artillery Brigade

Independent Units

- 6th Marine Brigade (Black-Dragon) on Baengnyeongdo island
- 9th Marine Brigade
- Yeon-Pyeong Unit on Yeonpyeong island

After the invasion by North Korean forces in 1950, the ROKMC was rapidly expanded to become an elite combat force. Once the Korean war was frozen in 1953 by the armistice, the south's military was able to be re-organised and re-trained for amphibious operations. The 1st Marine Division was established in 1955 and its units were routinely engaged in skirmishes with communist forces along the De-Militarized Zone, or DMZ.

At the request of the US, the ROKMC's Blue Dragon Brigade was despatched to Vietnam in the 1960s to fight alongside the US Marine Corps.

The modern ROKMC is 29,000 strong and is configured for amphibious operations and to be the country's strategic reserve. In 2010, ROKMC artillery units traded fire with North Korean guns during the Yeonpyeong incident. This prompted moves to further bolster the fighting power of the ROKMC.

In March 2016, the South Korean Defense Ministry announced the creation of a new regiment-sized Quick Manoeuvre Force, nicknamed 'Spartan 3000', consisting of 3,000 South Korean marines. It is held at readiness to deploy anywhere in the Korean Peninsula within 24 hours in case of an attack from the north.

ABOVE: South Korea's marines are considered an elite force and held in reserve to react rapidly to unexpected events.
(ROK ARMED FORCES)

LEFT: South Korea's 'Recon Marines' undergo intensive and rigorous training to prepare them to spearhead amphibious landings.
(ROK ARMED FORCES)

Taiwan

Republic of China Marine Corps

ABOVE: Taiwanese President Tsai Ing-wen reviews a ROC Marine Corps battalion in Kaohsiung in July 2020.
(OFFICE OF THE PRESIDENT)

BELOW: ROC marines in a speed boat practice recovering divers during a covert beach reconnaissance exercise.
(XUAN SHISHENG)

The Republic of China Marine Corps (ROCMC) was formed out of the Navy Sentry Corps in December 1914 on mainland China, by the country's then nationalist government. After fighting the Japanese between 1937 and 1945, the ROC forces then battled communist forces in the civil war. The communist Red Army emerged victorious, and the remnants of the ROC retreated to Formosa Island in 1949 - the territory now known as Taiwan.

The US gave the ROC financial and military support during the 1950s and 1960s and the ROCMC was reorganised along the lines of the US Marines Corps. At this time, the ROC leadership envisaged the ROCMC leading the liberation of the mainland from the communist troops of the People's Liberation Army (PLA). It was expanded into a two-division structure. In 1971, the US recognised Beijing as the sole government of China but it continued to provide military aid to Taiwan.

The ROCMC has since been re-organised into a rapid reaction force to counter any attempt by the PLA to invade and seize Taiwan. Its divisional structure has been disbanded and the remaining 10,000 marines are now grouped in three brigades. Two brigades have a regional response role, in the north and south of the main island, and the third brigade was designated as a national strategic reserve. The ROCMC has retained an amphibious capability to enable it to reinforce or re-take any of the 169 islands that the Taiwan government controls.

MARINE CORPS COMMAND

- 66th Marine Brigade 'Vanguard'
- 77th Marine Brigade 'Iron Guards
- 99th Marine Brigade 'Iron Force', Kaohsiung
- Amphibious Armour Group
- Combat Support Group
- Wuchiu Garrison Command
- Armed Force Joint Operation Training Base

Thailand

Royal Thai Marine Corps

Thailand has a long maritime tradition, and its navy formed its first unit of sea soldiers in the 19th century to serve aboard Royal Thai Navy ships.

The modern Royal Thai Marine Corps, or RTMC, was founded in 1932, when its first vehicle-borne battalion was formed with the assistance of the United States Marine Corps. It was expanded to a regiment in 1940 and during the Cold War period it was regularly deployed to the Laos and Cambodian border regions to deal with incursions by communist insurgents. US military assistance included deliveries of amphibious shipping and armoured amphibious assault vehicles. Further operations were carried out against the insurgents along the Malaysian border in the 1970s. More recent operations include disaster relief after the 2004 Tsunami and security assistance to Cambodia after civil unrest in 2003.

The RTMC have also taken part in United Nations peacekeeping and observer missions in Iraq, Burundi, Darfur, and Sudan.

The amphibious capabilities of the Thai navy expanded dramatically in the 1990s with the entry to service of the helicopter carrier, HTMS *Chakri Naruebet*. This century, the purchase of amphibious ships from Singapore and China have added to the combat potential of the RTMC.

The modern RTMC has some 23,000 personnel, who are grouped into three marine infantry regiments and several independent battalions, including units assigned to the elite King's Guard.

To support amphibious operations, it has a mix of US-supplied Assault Amphibious Vehicles AAVP-7A1 (formerly known as the LVTP-7) and Chinese provided Type 05 amphibious armoured vehicles.

ROYAL THAI MARINE CORPS

1st Marine Battalion, King's Guard

RTMC Marine Division

- 1st Marine Regiment
- 2nd Marine Regiment
- 3rd Marine Regiment
- 9th Infantry Battalion King's Guard
- Marine Artillery Regiment
- Reconnaissance Battalion (Force Recon Marine/Marine Special Force)
- Marine Assault Amphibian Vehicle Battalion

ABOVE: Royal Thai Marines conduct amphibious assault training with US Marines during a joint exercise at Hat Yao Beach in Thailand. (US DOD)

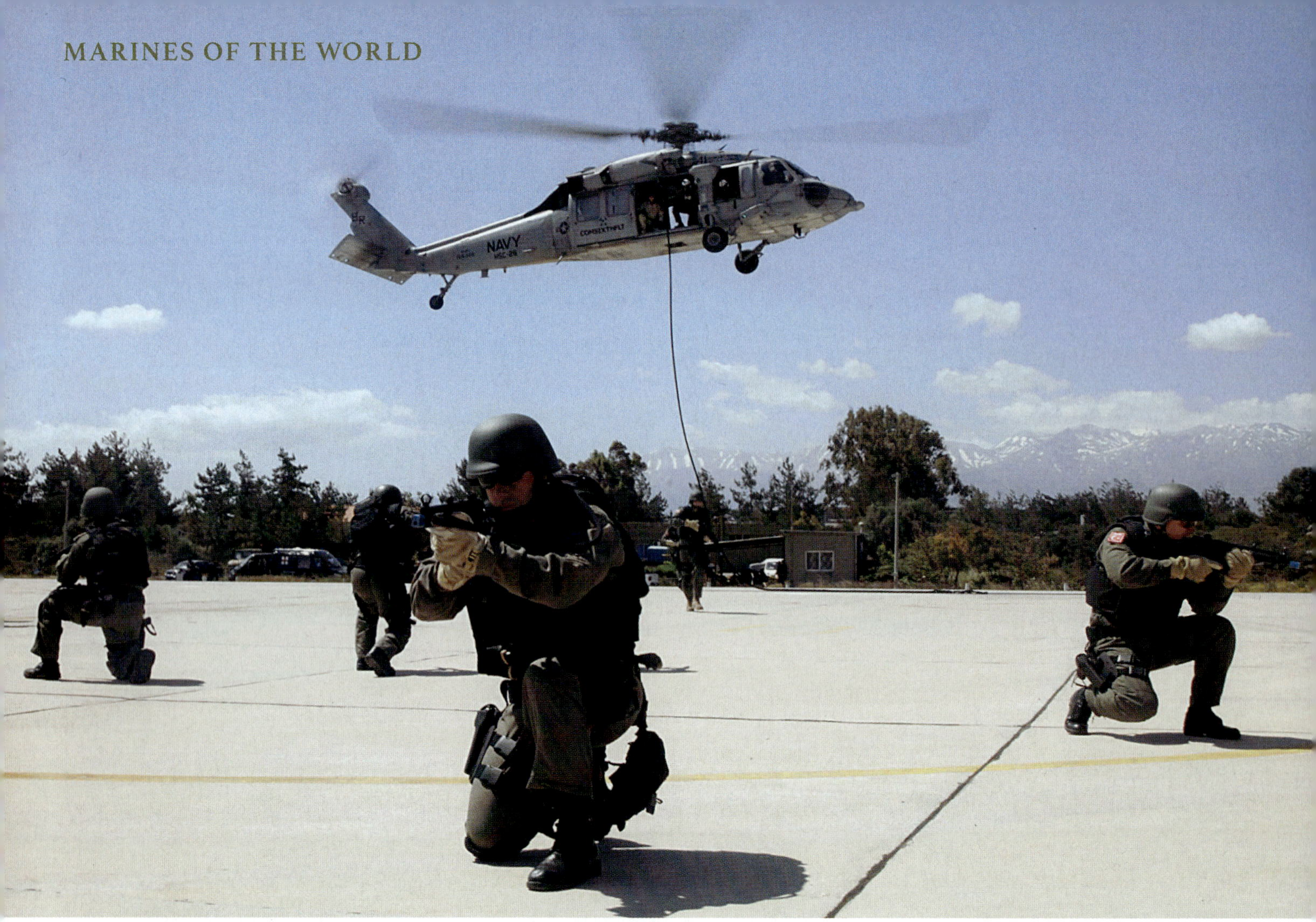

Turkey

Marine Infantry

ABOVE: Souda Bay, Greece (April 30, 2009) Turkish marines perform fast-rope exercises from a US Navy MH-60S Sea Hawk helicopter during an exercise with US forces. (US NAVY)

Turkey has a long tradition of amphibious operations stretching back to the time of the Byzantine and Ottoman empires. The modern Turkish Republic formed its first amphibious landing force, as part of the Turkish Naval Forces, in the 1960s with the help of US military aid after the country joined the NATO alliance.

In 1966 the Turkish Amphibious Group was formed, and it soon participated in NATO amphibious exercises with US and NATO forces in the Mediterranean region.

Further expansion continued, with the formation of 2nd Amphibious Marine Infantry Battalion in 1973 and the following year the 6th Amphibious Marine Infantry Regiment was stood up.

Tension with Greece over Cyprus escalated into all out war in July 1974, prompting Turkey to launch a major operation to seize the northern half of the island.

The Turkish 'Cakmak' Special Strike Force Landing Brigade carried out an amphibious landing at Pentemilli, after beach reconnaissance divers had judged it free of mines. The amphibious regiment secured the bridgehead and then fought some tough battles against Greek Cypriot forces until a cease fire was called.

In 1979, the 3rd Naval Infantry Battalion and an Amphibious Support Battalion were formed at Izmir to complete the brigade-sized landing force. During the 1990s, the marine units participated in UN and NATO peacekeeping missions in the Balkan region. Turkish amphibious ships and embarked marines took part in the evacuations of civilians from Albania in 1997 and Libya in 2011. Marine units also participated in the Turkish intervention in Syria in the land combat role.

RIGHT: Turkish marines boarding teams practice tactical movements aboard the frigate TCG *Gokceada* during Exercise Phoenix Express in Spain 2017. (US DOD)

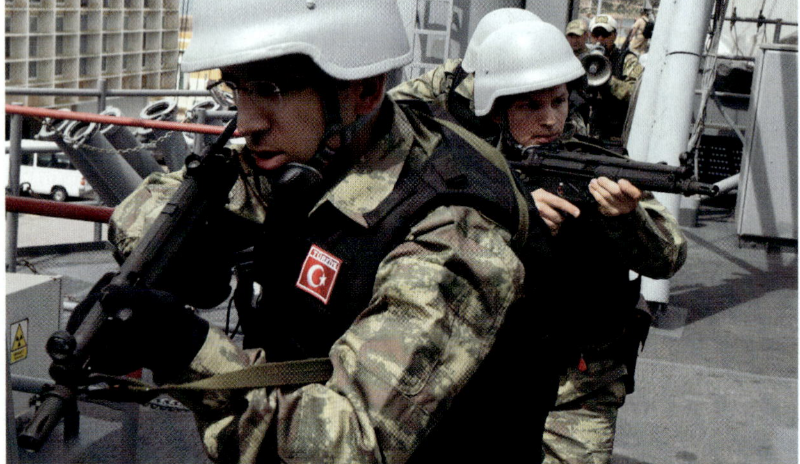

AMPHIBIOUS MARINE BRIGADE (FOÇA NEAR İZMIR)

- 1st Marine Infantry Battalion
- 2ndMarine Infantry Battalion
- 3rdMarine Infantry Battalion
- Tank Battalion
- Artillery Battalion
- Support Battalion

Ukraine

Marine Infantry of Ukraine

Ukraine's Marine Infantry, or Marine Corps, traces its roots back to the 880th Separate Naval Infantry Battalion of the old Soviet Black Sea Fleet, which transferred to the new Ukraine in 1994 after it gained its independence from the Soviet Union.

As a result of a series of budget cuts in the 1990s, the Ukrainian armed forces were shrunk dramatically and by 2014 there was only one naval infantry battalion left. This unit was based on Crimea when Russian forces seized the territory in 2014 and it ceased to exist after the majority of its personnel deserted to join the Russian military.

As a result, the Ukrainian navy ordered a major expansion of the marine forces and by the time of the Russian invasion in February 2022 there were two marine brigades, as well as several independent battalions, marine artillery, and coastal defence missile brigades. It boasted 6,000 personnel at this point.

The marine units were based in southern coastal regions to defend strategic positions when Russian forces invaded and were soon locked in heavy fighting. The 501st Battalion of the 36th Brigade was surrounded in the city of Mariupol and held out for more than six weeks before surrendering inside the Azoz steel works.

As western arms started to arrive in the summer and autumn of 2022, the marine brigades were re-equipped as elite assault units and sent to zones of intense combat. Hundreds of Ukrainian marines were flown to Britain to receive amphibious raiding training. Following this, they used their new skills to launch raids against Russian units in the Dnieper river delta and on Crimea, making use of robot craft in several attacks.

In May 2023, Ukrainian President Volodymyr Zelensky, in honour of the heroic actions of marine units, separated the force from the Ukrainian navy and designated it as Ukraine's fourth military branch.

MARINE INFANTRY OF UKRAINE

- 35th Marine Brigade
- 36th Marine Brigade
- 37th Marine Brigade
- 38th Marine Brigade
- 406th Marine Artillery Brigade
- 140th Force Reconnaissance Battalion
- 32nd Artillery Regiment
- 503rd Separate Marine Battalion

ABOVE: Ukrainian marines travelled to Britain in 2022 to undergo training in maritime raiding, ahead of returning to their country to take the fight to Russia on the Dnieper front. (MOD/CROWN COPYRIGHT)

LEFT: To win a place in the Ukrainian marines, recruits have to take part in a rigorous selection and training regime, including operating in small boats in littoral environments. (YEVHEN SILKIN/UKRAINIAN MINISTRY OF DEFENCE)

United Kingdom

Royal Marines

British naval captains long employed heavily armed men on their ships to enforce discipline and to act as landing parties on hostile coasts. Sir Francis Drake sometimes used infantry soldiers aboard his fleet as snipers in the rigging, but it was not until 1672 that the term 'marine' was officially used to denote the new maritime infantry.

The first official unit of marines was initially known as the Duke of Albany's Maritime Regiment and became the Admiral's Regiment on October 28, 1664, which is officially recognised as the founding day of the British Corps of Royal Marines. Later they became known as marines and in 1802 they were given the official Title of Royal Marines by King George III.

These early marines won their famous battle honour by helping to capture Gibraltar from Spain in 1704. Early marine units played an important part the American War of Independence and the establishment of the first British colonies in Australia. During the Imperial campaigns of the Victorian era, they become known as the Royal Marine Light Infantry.

RIGHT: It is the job of 47 (Raiding Group) Commando to land Royal Marines on hostile shores in raiding coats and landing craft. (MOD/CROWN COPYRIGHT)

BELOW: During 2023 the Royal Marines began training their Ukrainian counterparts to conduct raiding operations against Russian controlled coasts. (MOD/CROWN COPYRIGHT)

3 COMMANDO BRIGADE ROYAL MARINES, 2023

30 Commando Information Exploitation Group (Plymouth)

40 Commando (Taunton)

42 Commando (Bickleigh)

43 (Fleet Protection Group) Commando (Faslane)

45 Commando (Arbroath)

47 (Raiding Group) Commando (Plymouth)

Commando Logistic Regiment (Chivenor)

24 Commando Regiment, Royal Engineers (Chivenor)

29 Commando Regiment, Royal Artillery (Plymouth)

In World War One the Royal Marines played an important role in setting up the Royal Naval Division, which led the campaign to protect the Belgium port of Antwerp. They then took part in the ill-fated Gallipoli landings to secure the Dardanelles Straits near the Turkish capital Istanbul. In the first major commando raid of the 20th century, Royal Marines took part in the 1918 assault on the German controlled port of Zeebrugge in Belgium.

After British troops were driven from mainland Europe in 1940, the Royal Marines found themselves in the forefront of taking the fight back to Nazi controlled countries. The Royal Marine Division become the first large formation of troops trained in conducting amphibious landings and many of its personnel became the first crews of newly introduced landing craft.

These first commandos were originally part of the British Army established in 1941 on the orders of Winston Churchill. In 1942, units of Royal Marine infantry began converting to the new commando role subsequently taking part in the Dieppe and D-Day landings. Other Royal Marines were trained to carry out sabotage operations using small canoes, or kayaks, under the cover name of the Royal Marines Boom Patrol Detachment (RMBPD). These evolved into the Special Boat Section that carried out naval raids around the Mediterranean.

At the end of World War Two the British Army disbanded its commando units but the Royal Marines decided to permanently adopt the traditions of this elite force. The Royal Marines created a standing formation – 3 Commando Brigade - that was organised, equipped, and trained for amphibious operations. No longer would the Royal Navy have to reinvent its amphibious capability in a time of crisis, it would become a core competency of the British naval service. Projecting land power ashore would be the job of the Royal Marines. The Royal

ABOVE: Royal Marines undergo intense Arctic survival training before being allowed to operate in the far north of Norway. (MOD/CROWN COPYRIGHT)

BELOW: Merlin HC4 assault helicopters of the Royal Navy's Commando Helicopter Force support 3 Commando Brigade in all environments. (MOD/CROWN COPYRIGHT)

value of retaining a robust amphibious capability. The Royal Marines carried out a major amphibious assault to capture the Al Faw peninsula in the opening hours of the 2003 invasion of Iraq. Units of 3 Commando Brigade were employed in a land role in Afghanistan between 2002 and 2011.

The 2010 defence review reduced the readiness level of 3 Commando Brigade so that only one battalion-sized commando unit was to be held on alert, or at high readiness, to carry out amphibious operations at short notice. As a result, the size of the amphibious shipping fleet was reduced, saving considerable sums of money.

In the Future Commando Force initiative that got under way in 2017, the Royal Marines began to restructure 3 Commando Brigade away from predominately manoeuvre conventional combat operations to smaller scale missions in littoral environments.

The move away from battalion-sized operations coincided with the entry to service of the two Queen Elizabeth-class aircraft carriers, which have an air assault capability but not an amphibious role. The Royal Marines were mandated to provide embarked contingents on the two carriers whenever they sail able to conduct combat search and rescue missions to recover downed aircrew.

The old structure of having three battalion-sized commando units trained and equipped solely for amphibious operations also had to be adapted considerably. Each of the main commando units was given a specialist mission within the Future Commando Force structure.

40 Commando became the dedicated experimental and trials

Navy supported the Royal Marines by building and operating specialist amphibious shipping that was capable of launching landing craft carrying troops, vehicles, and stores.

The Royal Marines led the way in developing new amphibious warfare tactics, techniques, and equipment. In 1956 they carried out the first ever assault using helicopters to land troops ashore during the brief Suez campaign. After providing an amphibious rapid reaction force in the Far East and Middle East during the 1960s, 3 Commando Brigade was re-roled in the early 1970s to support NATO's northern flank in Norway.

3 Commando Brigade played a leading role in the 1982 Falkland campaign, and this dramatically demonstrated the

unit, with the remit to test new equipment, tactics, and techniques. The ultimate aim of these experimental efforts is to enable small groups of a few dozen Royal Marines to have the same combat effectiveness as old company sized contingents of over 100 troops. For example, employing swarms of mini-drones to allow a couple of Royal Marines to monitor dozens of square kilometres of ground without having hundreds of soldiers to physically occupy it.

42 Commando took on the maritime security role with its personnel providing small boarding and raiding detachments on board Royal Navy warships. The unit is mandated to provide embarked contingents on the two aircraft carriers able to conduct combat search and rescue missions, known as Joint Personnel Recovery (JPR), to recover downed aircrew whenever they sailed. It also provides maritime security teams to protect Royal Fleet Auxiliary support ships, and Point-class roll-on, roll off ships sailing in high threat regions.

45 Commando retained the conventional war fighting and amphibious role but with a focus on the high north of Norway and the Arctic region.

The Royal Marines landing craft and small boats are now grouped under 47 (Raiding Group) Commando, and they provide detachments to serve on amphibious ships or from shore bases.

30 Commando is the brigade's specialist reconnaissance, signals intelligence, and information analysis unit. It contains the Special Reconnaissance Squadron which

is trained and equipped to carry out covert beach reconnaissance on hostile coasts by submarine, boat, or air.

The Commando Logistic Regiment has the job of providing administrative, medical, logistic, motor transport and other support elements to deployed units of the brigade.

One unique unit within 3 Commando Brigade is 43 Commando which is the modern-day successor to the old Comacchio Company that was formed in the 1970s to protect North Sea oil rigs from terrorist attacks. It is now dedicated to protecting the UK nuclear deterrent both at its base at Faslane and the road convoys that move nuclear warheads to the

Atomic Weapons Establishment at Aldermaston.

The final element of 3 Commando Brigade are its attached British Army units that are trained to support amphibious operations.

The Commando Gunners of 29 Regiment Royal Artillery provide gun batteries with the 105mm Light Gun, they can be flown ashore by helicopter or moved by landing craft. They also provide forward artillery and air control teams to operate with commando units. These teams are experts at calling down fire support from 105mm Light Guns, naval gunfire support from warships, and air strikes by fast jets or helicopters gunships.

ABOVE: Royal Marines of 42 Commando have a maritime security role, providing force protection on board Royal Fleet Auxiliary vessels and specialist boarding teams on Royal Navy warships. (MOD/CROWN COPYRIGHT)

BELOW: In April 2023 Royal Marines of 40 Commando led the non-combatant evacuation operation to the Sudan to bring home British passport holders. (MOD/CROWN COPYRIGHT)

United States of America

ABOVE: Amphibious assault vehicles manoeuvre into the well deck of the assault ship USS *Bonhomme Richard*, during a training exercise prior to a deployment. (US NAVY)

The United States Marine Corps is the world's largest amphibious force. Its 180,000 personnel dwarf many other military services, and it is bigger than all but one European national armed force.

It is currently one of the five US armed services, and the Marine Corps commandant sits as a member of the US Joint Chiefs of Staff. For administrative purposes it is part of the Department of Navy. Its sister service, the US Navy, has an important role to play in delivering marine units to operational theatres on board amphibious shipping.

The corps traces its history back to November 10, 1775, when the Revolutionary Congress authorised the formation of the first units of Continental Marines to fight against the British in the American War of Independence. At the end of the war, the marines and other American military units were disbanded

RIGHT: A USMC F-35B Lightning II prepares to land on an amphibious assault ship. The new jet is replacing the veteran AV-8B Harrier in marine expeditionary units. (US NAVY)

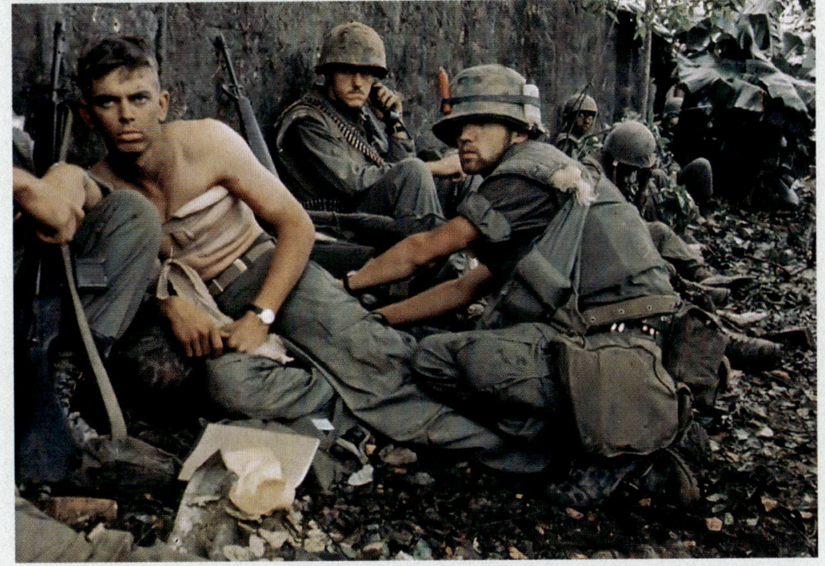

because the new United States did not want to pay for a standing military. This changed in August 1794 when US Congress created the regular US Navy and Marine Corps to protect America's maritime trade interests.

Detachments of marines served on US Navy ships throughout the 18th and 19th centuries in continuing clashes with British, Spanish, and French ships. When America fought a war with Berber pirates in North Africa, US Marines landed in Libya to earn their famous battle honour, Tripoli, that is immortalised in the corps' hymn.

In the 1847 American-Mexico war, marines led the US advance on Mexico City and stormed Chapultepec Castle to raise the stars and stripes over the fortress. Heavy losses, among marine officers and non-commissioned officers is memorialised in corps dress uniform trousers' 'blood stripes'.

In World War One, marine units were landed in France to serve on the Western Front as part of the American Expeditionary Force. They were soon in the thick of the action and this significantly enhanced their reputation as an elite fighting force. At the Battle of Belleau Wood in June 1918, the marines held their ground in the face of a German offensive, in response to the rallying cry, "Retreat? Hell, we just got here!"

During the 1930s the corps underwent a major reorganisation to turn it into a specialist amphibious force, under the Fleet Marine Force initiative. This saw the expansion of the corps into the air, land, and sea organisation that exists today, The first specialist landing craft were developed, and marine aviation units were expanded.

US MARINE CORPS HYMN

From the Halls of Montezuma
To the shores of Tripoli
We fight our country's battles
In the air, on land, and sea
First to fight for right and freedom
And to keep our honor clean
We are proud to claim the Title
Of United States Marine.

Our flag's unfurled to every breeze
From dawn to setting sun
We have fought in ev'ry clime and place
Where we could take a gun
In the snow of far-off Northern lands
And in sunny tropic scenes
You will find us always on the job
The United States Marines.

Here's health to you and to our Corps
Which we are proud to serve
In many a strife we've fought for life
And never lost our nerve
If the Army and the Navy
Ever look on Heaven's scenes
They will find the streets are guarded
By United States Marines.

ABOVE LEFT: The Battle of Hue in 1968 was the toughest fight the US Marine Corps faced during the long Vietnam conflict. (USMC)

BELOW: US Marines played a pivotal role in the World War Two Pacific campaign, capturing a string of islands in the face of fanatical Japanese resistance. (US NATIONAL ARCHIVES)

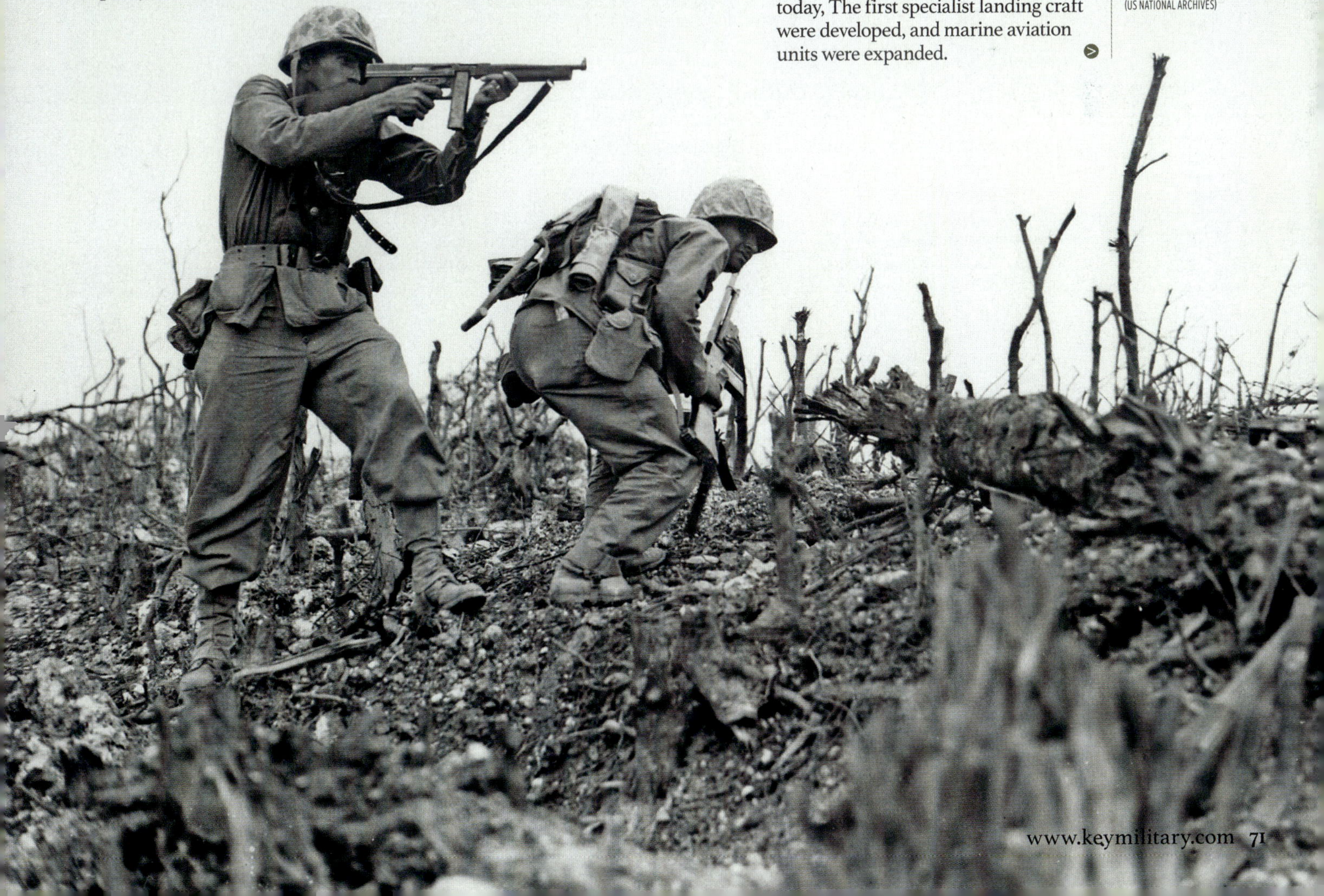

ABOVE: US Marines searching Saddam Hussein's palace in Baghdad in April 2003 after spearheading the advance in the Iraqi capital. (US DOD)

After the Japanese surprise attack on the US Pacific fleet at Pearl Harbor in December 1941, the corps was expanded to spearhead the US island-hopping campaign across the Pacific. US Marines stormed ashore on several heavily defended Japanese islands and fought bloody battles to capture them. The names of these islands – Guadalcanal, Iwo Jima, Peleliu, Tarawa, Saipan, and Okinawa - are now immortalised as corps battle honours and several US Navy amphibious ships have borne their names.

Since World War Two, the corps has been America's main rapid reaction force and has seen action in almost every war or intervention over the past 75 years.

Marine Expeditionary Force

The modern US Marine Corps operates as a combined arms force, bringing together air, land, and sea forces under a single commander to achieve their objectives.

This is the modern-day successor of the Fleet Marine Force that allowed the marines to achieve victory in World War Two. The corps uses the Marine Air-Ground Task Force (MAGTF) concept to organise its units at every level of operations.

A MAGTF is composed of four elements: the command element (CE), the ground combat element (GCE), the aviation combat element (ACE) and the logistics combat element (LCE). Each MAGTF can operate independently or as part of a large US or coalition force. They are temporary commands that are formed for a specific mission and dissolved after completion of that mission.

A MAGTF varies in size from the smallest, a Marine Expeditionary Unit (MEU), based around a reinforced infantry battalion and a composite aviation squadron, up to the largest, a Marine Expeditionary Force (MEF). A MEF is equivalent to an army corps-sized formation, which brings together a marine

ground division, an air wing, and a logistics group under a USMC lieutenant general.

The modern USMC is structured as a force generation organisation to provide deployable units to theatre or regional combatant commanders for training exercises, routine deployment, or combat operations.

The two peacetime MEFs are based in the continental United States and a third is forward deployed in Japan. Each MEF operates on a readiness cycle to generate forces that are trained and equipped for overseas operations to specific time lines.

Currently each year, one or two MEUs are generated to serve aboard Amphibious Ready Groups (ARG) that forward deploy to Europe, the Middle East, and Far East. These serve six months at a time and stand ready to conduct a range of missions, including non-combatant evacuation operations (NEOs).

To provide more crisis coverage, over the past decade, Special Purpose Marine Air-Ground Task Forces,

Crisis Response (SPMAGTF-CR) have been formed at land bases in the Middle East and in the Mediterranean to deploy by helicopter and aircraft to incidents, such as the NEO mission to Kabul in Afghanistan in August 2021.

For major crisis, such as the 1991 and 2003 Iraq wars, full MEF-sized formations of marines have been deployed. These operate as corps-sized manoeuvre formations, fighting alongside the US Army. In 2003, the I Marine Expeditionary Force led the US advance on Baghdad.

For the counter insurgency campaign in Afghanistan, a divisional-sized MAGTF operated alongside British forces to control Helmand Province from 2010 to 2014. Units from across the US Marine Corps rotated into Afghanistan to sustain the fight against the Taliban.

The corps has long been a professional service and it has a formidable reputation as a fighting force. This is due in part to the tough training regime that its recruits undergo and the professionalism of its officers. Perhaps the most famous modern USMC officer is General Jim Mattis, who rose to be the top US commander in the Middle East and US secretary of defense from 2017 to 2019 under President Donald Trump. He reputedly selected Mattis to head the Pentagon after hearing he was nicknamed 'Mad Dog', on account of his aggressive battlefield tactics.

America's 911 Force

When a crisis erupts anywhere in the world, the President of the United States first dispatches an aircraft carrier and then his next move is to order a Marine Expeditionary Unit, or MEU, to sail to the sound of battle. It is not surprising that MEUs are often nicknamed 'America's 911 Force', after the telephone number for American police and other blue light emergency services.

The full title of these units is Marine Expeditionary Unit (Special Operations Capable), or MEU (SOC), and they are some of the most high-profile parts of the US military.

A MEU (SOC) is a self-contained intervention force of 2,200 Marines, who are embarked on a small task group of specialist amphibious shipping, known as an Amphibious ❯

BELOW: US Marine Corps regularly train with French forces in the east African country of Djibouti, as part of on-going engagement with regional armed forces. (USMC)

ABOVE: The AAVP-7A1 (formerly the LVTP-7) is the US Marine Corps Assault Amphibious Vehicle. It is the modern successor of the World War Two Alligator amphibious tractor. (USMC)

BELOW: In 2010, the US Marines spearheaded the surge of US forces into Afghanistan in a bid to turn back the Taliban insurgent offensive. (USMC)

AV-8B Harrier or F-35B Lightning jump jets, forming the aviation combat element
• A combat logistics battalion providing the logistics element

A USMC colonel usually commands a MEU (SOC), but the ARG or ESG are led by US Navy admirals. The elements of the MEU(SOC) are embarked across the three ships of the ARG, which usually comprise a flat top amphibious assault ship, a transport dock ship, and a landing dock ship. These ships usually act as the home base for the ARG's landing craft and hovercraft, which are dubbed landing craft air cushion, or LCACs.

The US Marine Corps has to generate fully trained and equipped MEU (SOC) to meet the requirements set by the Joint Chiefs of Staff and regional combatant commanders around the world. For most of 2022 and 2023, the US Marine Corps and US Navy was required to have one MEU(SOC) at sea in the Pacific or Indian Ocean regions and another carrying out training close to its home port. Two other MEU(SOC)s were held at readiness to sail within a week or so of getting a call to arms.

A decade ago, at the height of the 'Global War on Terror', the USMC generated three or four MEU(SOC)s at a time with two usually deployed in the Middle East or Mediterranean, as well as one being at sea in the Pacific region.

Ready Group, or ARG. When combined with escorting warships, submarines, and patrol aircraft they are known as an Expeditionary Strike Group, or ESG.

Each MEU (SOC) is a self-contained amphibious force that is able to deploy by ship, landing craft, or aircraft to a crisis zone. It has its own integral ground combat units, aviation support and landing crafts.

The USMC elements, normally comprise:

• A reinforced infantry battalion, designated as a battalion landing team or ground combat element
• A composite aviation squadron, of MV-22B tilt-rotors, CH-53E heavy lift helicopters, AH-1Z Cobra helicopter gunships, UH-1Y Huey utility helicopters,

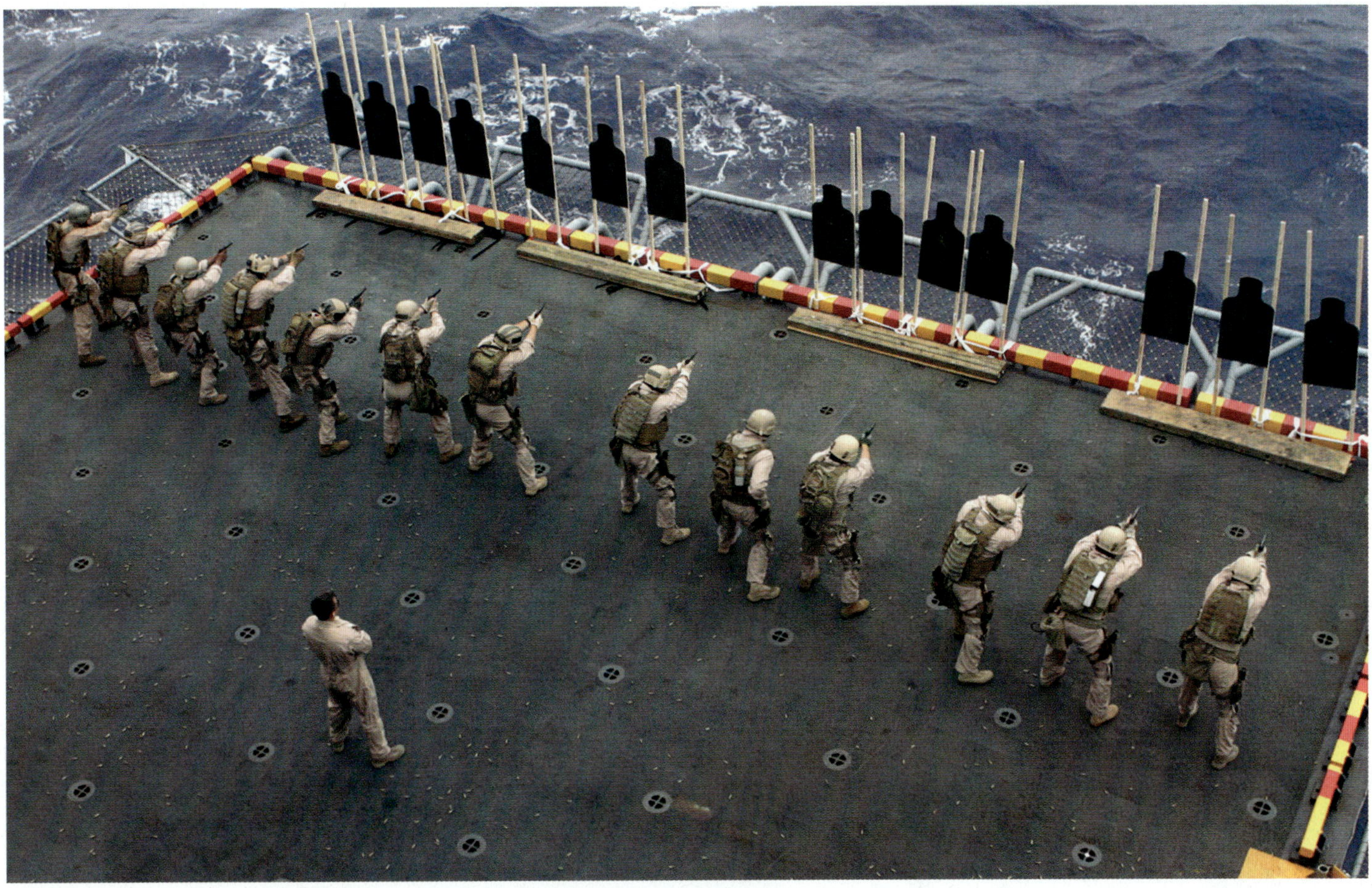

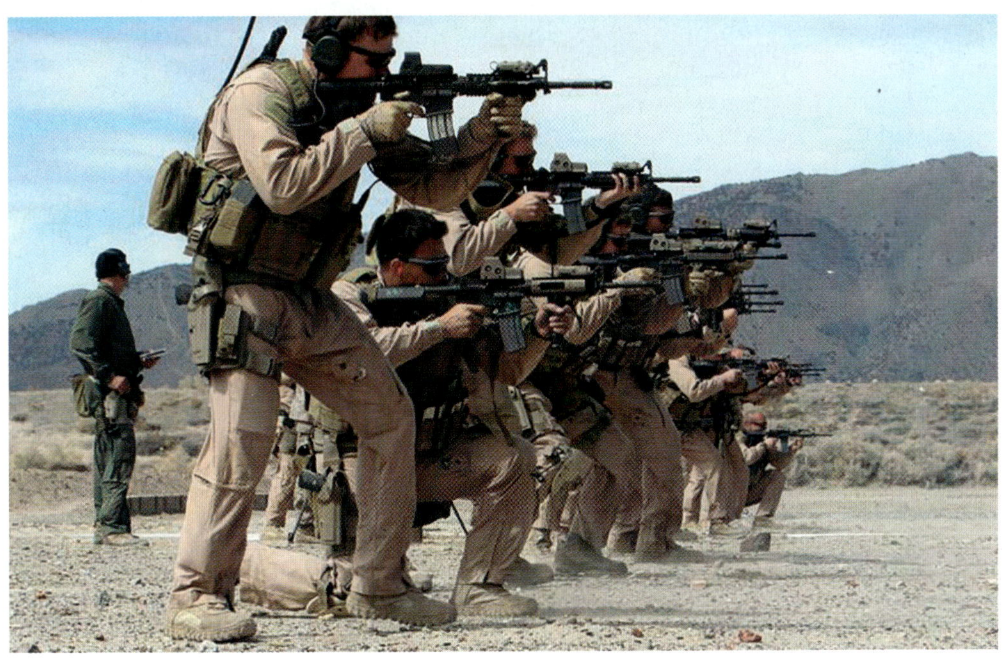

I MARINE EXPEDITIONARY FORCE (CAMP PENDLETON, CALIFORNIA)
I Marine Expeditionary Force (Camp Pendleton, California) • 11th MEU(SOC) • 13th MEU(SOC) • 15th MEU (SOC) II Marine Expeditionary Force (Camp Lejeune, North Carolina) • 22nd MEU(SOC) • 24th MEU (SOC) • 26th MEU (SOC) III Marine Expeditionary Force (Camp Smedley D. Butler, Okinawa, Japan) • 31st MEU (SOC)

The composition and high readiness of MEU(SOC) means they are often called on to react to situations were US citizens need to be evacuated from crisis or conflict zones. These non-combatant evacuation operations, or NEOs, are often high profile and show off the capabilities of the modern US Marine Corps in a positive light. These capabilities are also very welcome if a MEU (SOC) is called to provide humanitarian assistance following natural disasters.

US Marine Corps – Aviation

The US Marine Corps is unique among the world's amphibious forces in having its own integral aviation branch. It currently boasts more than 300 fast jet combat aircraft and more than 800 helicopters. This is bigger than many air forces and means US Marines never have to want for air support when they go into battle.

The first USMC aviation units were formed after World War One and a little over 20 years later there were 145 squadrons supporting marines in the battles of the Pacific campaign.

Although USMC aviators are trained at US Navy flight schools, they have to first pass the marines basic officer or recruit training. They are marines first, aviators second. This ethos is the key to ensuring marine aviation is

ABOVE: US Marines maintain their shooting skills from the stern deck of a US Navy warship. (US NAVY)

BELOW: Marines of the 2nd Marine Special Operations Battalion are a dedicated unit for unconventional warfare and counter-terrorist missions. (USMC)

ABOVE: The F-35B Lightning II jump jet is now in widespread use with the USMC, with more than 120 currently in service. (US NAVY)

always overhead when marines are fighting on the ground.

USMC aviation units are configured to operate across a spectrum of tactical scenarios as amphibious operations unfold. In the first phase, USMC units must be able to operate from a range of US Navy warships. The Hornet squadrons are trained to fly off US Navy aircraft carriers to strike at targets far behind enemy lines. Close air support is the job of the AV-8B Harrier, F-35B Lightning jump jets and AH-1Z Cobra helicopter gunships embarked on assault ships.

Moving the landing force ashore is the job of the MV-22B Osprey tilt-rotors, CH-53E Sea Stallion heavy lift helicopters and UH-1Y Huey utility helicopters. They also help in moving supplies into beachheads and evacuating wounded personnel. The MV-22B is unique to the USMC and it can carry marines on long distance missions, with their range being extended by air-to-air refuelling from USMC KC-130J Hercules tanker aircraft.

When the amphibious force lands ashore, the aviation support moves

RIGHT: The MV-22B Osprey tilt rotor can take off and land like a helicopter but then transition to conventional flight. (US NAVY)

ABOVE: The USMC expects to retire its last AV-8B Harrier in 2025 to make way for more than 300 F-35B stealth aircraft. (US NAVY)

ashore to operate from forward airfields. Naval Construction Battalions, or Seabees, are trained and equipped to work with USMC combat engineers to rapidly build airfields, fuel tanks and ammunition dumps in combat zones. The USMC has air traffic control teams, aircraft technicians, logistic support, and security teams to ensure flight operations can continue at a high tempo.

USMC aviation units are also configured to operate in a range of configurations, from small independent squadrons assigned to a MEU (SOC). This later type of unit combines several types of aircraft and helicopters under a single commander, and they are usually embarked on an amphibious assault ship or helicopter carrier.

During a large-scale operation, several squadrons can be combined into marine air groups that deploy to overseas theatres of operations. In the 1991 and 2003 Gulf Wars, full Marine Expeditionary Forces were deployed to the Middle East and their aviation element comprised a full marine air wing, with the full spectrum of combat aviation units.

In these large wars, the US military has tried to centralise control of all US air units in an operational theatre under a single air component headquarters to direct air power for strategic effect. To ensure USMC doctrine of marine airpower being directed by USMC commanders is applied successfully, the USMC assigns officers to the centralised air headquarters to co-ordinate air operations and ensure marine aviation is allocated to support sectors of the battlefield where marine ground units are fighting.

BELOW: Logistic support and troop transport missions are carried out by the veteran CH-53E Sea Stallion heavy lift helicopters. (US NAVY)

Putting Marines on the Beach

Modern Amphibious Shipping

RIGHT: Many amphibious ships have a well deck that allows landing craft to dock safely inside. Here the amphibious assault ship USS *Iwo Jima* prepares to receive landing craft. (US NAVY)

Delivering troops, vehicles and other heavy equipment to shore requires specialised ships and other craft. They must be designed to navigate across shallow water to beaches and they usually have ramps to allow the rapid unloading of personnel or vehicles.

As a result of the rapid expansion of British and American amphibious forces during World War Two, whole families of specialist craft were developed to put troops ashore on Pacific Islands and the coast of Nazi occupied Europe. These were broadly split into landing craft designed to actually land troops or vehicles, and those intended to move amphibious forces - both landing craft and assault troops - across oceans to the vicinity of their objectives. The two scenarios required very different designs to deal with sea conditions in coastal regions and those far out at sea. Landing craft needed flat bottoms to get in close to shore, whereas ocean going vessels needed conventional shaped hulls to ensure their passengers and cargo could endure several weeks at sea, often in stormy conditions. This division of types of amphibious shipping still operates today. During World War Two, the Royal Navy and US Navy devised a system for designating types of amphibious vessels and this system remains in use. Under this system the role of the craft was always used after the words 'landing craft'. So, landing craft designed to carry tanks were called landing craft tank, which was shortened to LCT.

Landing Craft and Ships

The first vessels that we would recognise as landing craft were developed after World War One as a result of the disastrous Gallipoli landings. These were flat bottomed and featured a bow ramp, which could be dropped to allow troops to disembark rapidly on beaches.

In the first years of World War Two, the size and capabilities of landing craft were rapidly expanded. The

BELOW: The French Navy amphibious assault ship FS *Mistral* underway in the Mediterranean Sea. She is a multi-role platform, capable of operating helicopters and landing craft. (US NAVY)

LEFT: A landing craft inside the well deck of HMAS *Canberra*. (ROYAL AUSTRALIAN NAVY)

BELOW: Royal Marine landing craft depart at speed from HMS *Albion*. (MOD/CROWN COPYRIGHT)

need to put tanks ashore meant that landing craft got bigger to accommodate armoured vehicles. Specialist versions equipped with weapons to provide fire support to beach landings were then developed, as well as command post and medical evacuation versions. Water jet propulsion was an added feature to avoid snagging propellers on rocks or underwater vegetation.

Landing craft are generally not designed to be ocean going but the need to carry vehicles over long distances has led to the development of landing ships, with flat bottoms and bow doors. This allows them to approach beaches and then unload their vehicles directly on to the shoreline. They share many design characteristics with civilian roll-on, roll-off ferries. Their biggest difference is reinforced hulls to survive being beached, anchoring systems to hold them in place during unloading, and azimuth thrusters to allow them to manoeuvre in shallow water.

The invention of hovercraft was identified as having great potential in amphibious warfare and several navies have adopted them. The US designated them Landing Craft Air Cushion, or LCACs. Large ones are used to carry vehicles and smaller versions are used for the tactical movement of personnel across soft beaches or marshy terrain.

Dock Ships

The proliferation of landing craft types in World War Two led to consideration being given to how to get them to the amphibious operational area, so they could

ABOVE: The Engin de Débarquement amphibie rapide (EDA-R) is a class of French roll-on/roll-off catamaran landing craft (L-CAT) operated by the French and Egyptian navies. (US NAVY)

BELOW: Project 775 landing ships are the most numerous landing ships in the Russian fleet. Here is the RFS *Kaliningrad*. (RUSSIAN MINISTRY OF DEFENCE)

actually deliver troops ashore. This was particularly a problem for the US Marine Corps which had to sail thousands of miles from its home bases to land on Japanese-held islands in the central Pacific.

The initial solution was to convert flat decked train ferries into ships to carry landing craft. They would then be launched down a ramp/chute off the stern or lifted into the water by crane. However, the process was slow and became difficult in high sea states so toward the end of World War Two the first dock ships started to appear. These had a large internal dock called a well deck, with a large gate at the stern of the ship that could

be closed to allow the vessel to sail at speed in the open sea. Landing craft can be stored in the well deck during voyages and vehicles or personnel loaded onto them from a cargo or vehicle deck. This allows the whole cargo loading procedure to be carried out under cover and then a fully loaded landing craft can exit from the open stern dock gate. Amphibious armoured vehicles or LCACs can also be launched from the dock.

Larger landing dock ships also usually have a helicopter deck to allow movement of personnel or cargo by air. A command centre is also usually incorporated so landing operations can be co-ordinated from the ship.

Helicopter Carriers

The incorporation of helicopters into amphibious operations during the 1950s and 1960s led to the development of specialist ships to support them. The Royal Navy first used converted World War Two era 'flat top' aircraft carriers to launch a mass helicopter assault during the 1956 Suez crisis, and it soon formalised the idea by creating what were called 'commando carriers'.

In the early 1960s the US Navy fielded the first dedicated amphibious assault ships,or Landing Platform Helicopter (LPH), that were optimised to carry 1,800 US Marines and more than 20 helicopters to lift them ashore. However, they initially did not have an internal dock to allow the launching of landing craft. These ships were bigger than World War Two aircraft carriers. They were optimised around helicopters, featuring lifts big enough to carry the large transport helicopters and hangers high enough accommodate them. The ships were also designed with cabins to accommodate hundreds of marines, their weapons and equipment.

The first of these Iwo Jima-class vessels – the USS Iwo Jima - saw service in the Vietnam conflict and the experience led to the development in the 1970s of flat top assault ships, which also incorporated a well deck. These Landing Helicopter Assault (LHA) ships were true multi-role vessels that could launch marines ashore by air, landing craft or LCAC. They were also modified to allow the operation of the AV-8A/B Harrier jump jet so that fixed wing fast jets could be provide close air support for amphibious assaults.

Several other nations followed the US Navy's lead in developing multi-role amphibious assault ships. However, these vessels are some of the most complex warships in modern navies and as a result they are very expensive to build and operate. Some navies tried to cut costs by not going for a full working dock, with the 1990s-era British helicopter carrier HMS *Ocean* featuring only a stern ramp that had to be lowered to allow troops and vehicles to transfer to landing craft. The ship's landing craft were carried on davits, underneath the overhang of the flight deck. This meant that landing craft could not be loaded and launched in rough seas.

ABOVE: Hovercraft of 539 Assault Squadron Royal Marines were used to patrol around the port of Umm Qasr during the 2003 invasion of Iraq. The hovercraft have since been retired by the Royal Marines. (MOD/CROWN COPYRIGHT)

BELOW: The crews of British landing craft are provided by the Royal Marines of 47 Commando (Raiding Group). (MOD/CROWN COPYRIGHT)

Algeria

Algerian Naval Forces

The Algerian navy significantly expanded its amphibious shipping capability a decade ago when the ANS *Kalaat Beni Abbes* was commissioned. The 8,000-ton amphibious dock ship is an improved version of the San Giorgio-class, built by the Italian firm Fincantieri.

The ship has a continuous 'flattop' flight deck with two deck-landing spots for helicopters at the bow and stern. It has a dock to the rear which allows it to launch up to three landing craft. They can be loaded from the ship's internal well deck. Three additional landing craft, and two fast patrol boats can be launched from davits. The ship is normally supported by three Chaland-class landing craft, also built by Fincantieri, which can each carry a tank or a maximum of 140 personnel.

The ship can load up to 15 main battle tanks or large trucks and has accommodation for 440 marines, as well as 150 crew. A 60-bed hospital and operating theatres are also carried.

The ANS *Kalaat Beni Abbes* is augmented by two Kalaat Beni Hammed-class landing ships, the ANS *Kalaat Beni Hammed* and ANS *Kalaat Beni Rached*. These 80-metre-long vessels were originally built in the UK in the 1980s and have recently been modernised.

KALAAT BÉNI ABBÈS – AMPHIBIOUS TRANSPORT DOCK

Displacement: 8,800 tons

Length: 469ft (142.9m)

Beam: 71ft (21.5m)

Draught: 17ft (5.3m)

Propulsion: Two × Wärtsilä diesel engines

Speed: 20kts (37 kph; 23mph)

Range: 8,100 miles (13,000km)

Crew/Complement: 52 crew, 450 marines

Armament: 1 OTO Melara 76mm/62 SR Super Rapido, 2 × OTO Melara Oerlikon KBA 25mm/80, 8-cell SYLVER A50 VLS for 8 Aster 15&30 missiles (1x8 more A50 VLS FFBNW)

Aircraft carried: 3 x AW101 transport helicopters or 5 x Super Lynx helicopters

Aviation facilities: Hangar for recovery of Super Lynx helicopters

BELOW: ANS ship *Kalaat Beni-Abbes* took part the US-led exercise Phoenix Express in May 2016 to practice maritime safety and security in the Mediterranean. (US NAVY)

Argentina

Armada de la República Argentina

Argentina's amphibious shipping has been in a state of decline for more than 20 years. The country's economy has not been able to generate the funding needed to buy replacements for the amphibious ships that saw service during the Falklands conflict in the 1980s.

The Argentine Navy currently operates only one amphibious cargo ship, the ARA *Bahía San Blas*, but she is not a landing ship with opening bow doors and a vehicle ramp. Any vehicles or landing craft have to be carried inside the ship's three cargo holds and then lifted out by Liebherr cranes. She has a bulk cargo capacity of 6,300 tons and can carry up to 140 containers.

ARA *Bahía San Blas* is one of three Costa Sur-class cargo ships ordered by the Argentine Navy in 1975. They were designed and built by the Argentine Príncipe shipyard in Buenos Aires. One of the ships is up for sale and the other is used to re-supply Argentine bases in the Antarctic region.

In 1992, ARA *Bahía San Blas* transported back four Baradero-class patrol boats used by the United Nations monitoring mission in

Central America. After the retirement of the last landing ship, ARA *Cabo San Antonio*, in 1997, ARA *Bahía San Blas* became the main vessel used to deploy Argentine Marines. She received several modifications for this role.

Since 2004, the ship carried the Argentine contingent to Haiti to join the United Nations peacekeeping force on the Caribbean island and has completed several voyages to deliver personnel and equipment to it.

ARA *BAHÍA SAN BLAS* – AMPHIBIOUS CARGO VESSEL

Displacement: 10,894 tons

Length: 393ft (19.9m)

Beam: 57ft (17.5m)

Draught: 24.6ft (7.49m)

Propulsion: Two Sulzer 6 ZL 40/48 diesel engines

Speed max: 16.3kts (30.2kph)

Cargo capacity: 6,800 tons

Complement: 40

ABOVE: For the Argentine invasion of the Falklands in 1982 the tank landing ship, ARA *Cabo San Antonio*, delivered LVTP-7 to a beach near Port Stanley. The ship was scrapped in 1997 as part of a major run down of Argentina's amphibious capability. (MALVINAS VETERANS ASSOCIATION)

BELOW: Argentina now has only one working amphibious vessel, the ARA *Bahía San Blas*, which relies on cranes to unload vehicles and cargo. (MARIO ALBERTO ROMANUTTI)

Australia

Royal Australian Navy

They are the largest vessels ever operated by the Royal Australian Navy with a displacement of 27,500 tonnes. Each ship can embark up to 1,046 soldiers and there are facilities for a command element.

The ships have two vehicle decks (one for light vehicles, the other for heavy vehicles and tanks), and between them can accommodate up to 110 vehicles.

The heavy vehicle deck may alternately be used for cargo, with a capacity of 196 shipping containers. Each ship has a 69.3m by16.8m well deck, which houses up to four landing craft.

The flight deck has landing space for six helicopters up to MRH-90 size and the hangar deck can accommodate eight medium-size helicopters. An additional ten can be carried if the light vehicle deck is used as additional helicopter space. Two aircraft lifts connect the flight and hangar decks.

In 2010, the Bay-class landing ship dock, RFA *Largs Bay,* was put up for sale by the British Royal Navy and she was bought by Australia, entering service down under in 2011 as HMAS *Choules.*

ABOVE: The HMAS *Canberra* off the coast of Queensland, Australia, during Exercise Talisman Sabre 21, with US MH-60 helicopters embarked. (USAF)

BELOW: HMAS *Choules* was bought from Britain, after she was put up for sale in 2010. (SABERWYN)

The Royal Australian Navy launched a project at the turn of the century to re-build its amphibious landing capability to enhance the country's ability to project power across the Pacific region.

After an international competition, a design proposed by the Spanish company Navantia was selected in 2007. This is the same design used on the Spanish navy's ESPS *Juan Carlos I*. The ships have Australian-specific communications and other specialist equipment and are known as the Canberra-class. HMAS *Canberra* was commissioned in 2014 and her sister ship, HMAS *Adelaide*, entered service a year later.

Brazil

Marinha do Brasil

The Brazilian navy has the largest amphibious capability in South America following a campaign to buy up second-hand vessels from the US, UK, and France. These vessels saw long service with the previous owners so the ships will soon need major overhaul and modernisation to keep them serviceable beyond the end of this decade.

Brazil has ambitious plans to expand its naval power, including the building of nuclear-powered attack submarines, but new amphibious ships are not currently in the future ship building plan. This puts a long-term question mark over the fate of Brazil's amphibious landing force.

The flag ship of the Brazilian navy is the 'flat top' helicopter carrier *Atlântico,* which was previously HMS *Ocean* in Royal Navy service. She was sold to Brazil in 2018, after seeing active service in the 2003 Iraq invasion and the 2011 Libyan intervention.

Brazil's Foudre-class landing ship, the *Bahia,* was bought from France in 2015, after seeing service as the FS *Siroco.* She has a stern well deck to allow landing craft to be loaded internally.

The landing force is augmented by two tank landing ships (LST). The ex-British Round Table-class LST, RFA *Sir Bedivere,* was sold to Brazil in 2009 and entered service as the *Amirante Sabóia.* Her sister ship, the former RFA *Sir Galahad,* was also sold to Brazil in 2007 and served as the *Garcia D'Avila,* until she was retired in 2019. The ex-US Navy Newport-class landing ship, USS *Cayuga,* was bought by Brazil in 2001 and saw service until early in 2023, when she was retired.

ABOVE: The former HMS *Ocean* in is now the Brazilian navy flag ship, as the *Atlântico.* (BRAZILIAN NAVY)

BELOW: The *Atlântico* embarks an air group of HU-2 Super Cougars. (BRAZILIAN NAVY)

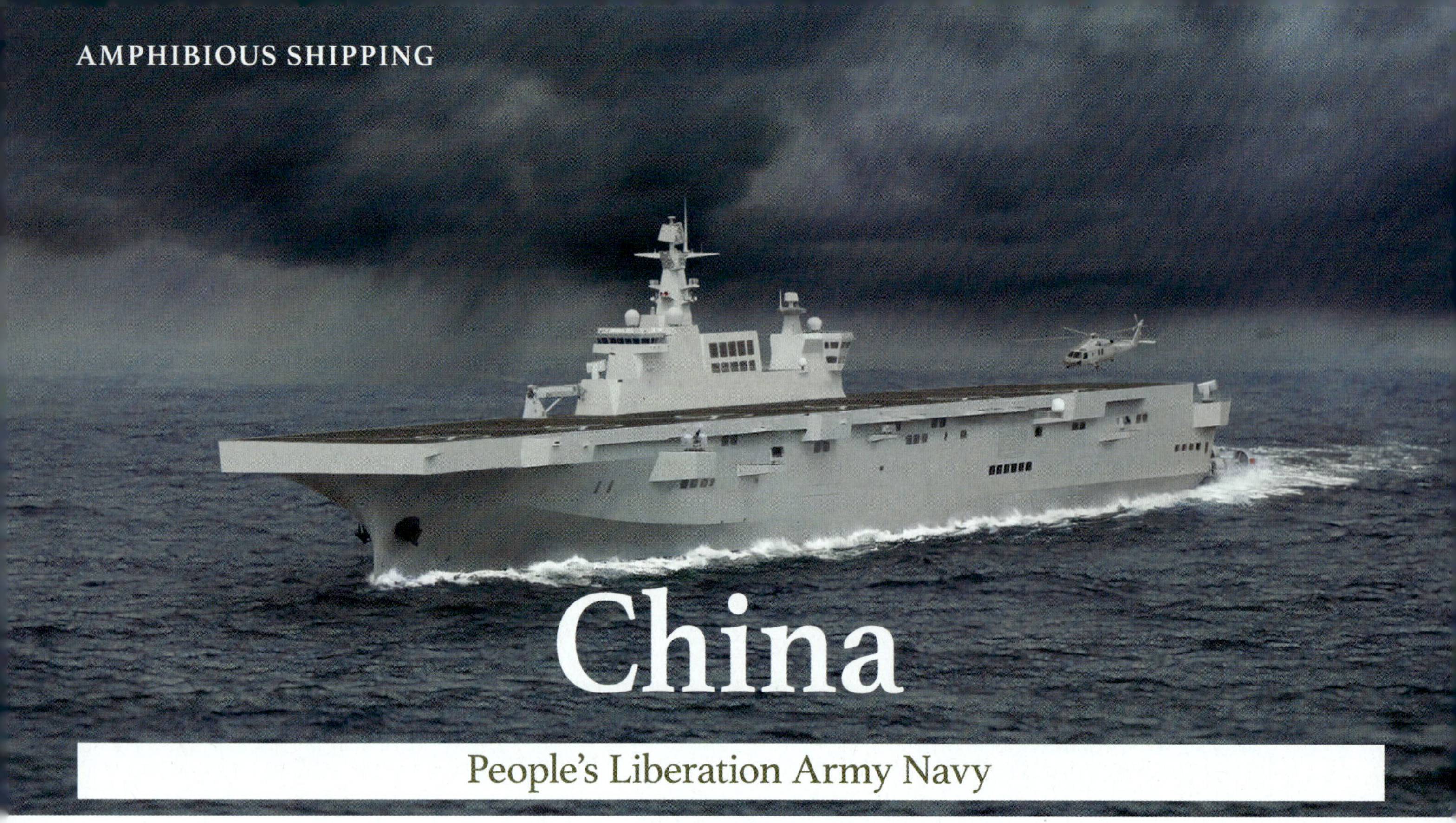

China

People's Liberation Army Navy

ABOVE: The Type 075 amphibious assault ships are the future flag ships of PLAN amphibious task forces. (XINGHAI MILITARY)

BELOW: A dozen Type 074-class landing ships built in the mid 1990s are operated by the PLAN. (TKSTEVEN)

The People's Liberation Army Navy (PLAN) is building up one of the world's most capable amphibious flotillas to project the PLAN Marine Corps ashore. This includes more than 50 amphibious vessels, including three helicopter carriers, eight dock ships, 40 landing ships, supported by 18 large landing craft, and 40 large hovercraft.

During its first 50 years the Chinese communist navy was focused on coastal operations and preparing for conflict with Taiwan. Its amphibious shipping was generally flat-bottomed

TYPE 071 CLASS - AMPHIBIOUS TRANSPORT DOCK SHIP

Displacement: 25,000 tons full load

Length: 689ft (210m)

Beam: 91ft 10in (28m)

Draft: 23ft (7m)

Speed: 25kts (46kph)

Range: 10,000nm (19,000km)

Capacity: 60 armoured fighting vehicles, 800 troops

Armament: One × AK-176 76mm (3in) gun, 4 × AK-630 30mm (1.2in) CIWS

Aircraft carried: Four x Z-8 Super Frelon

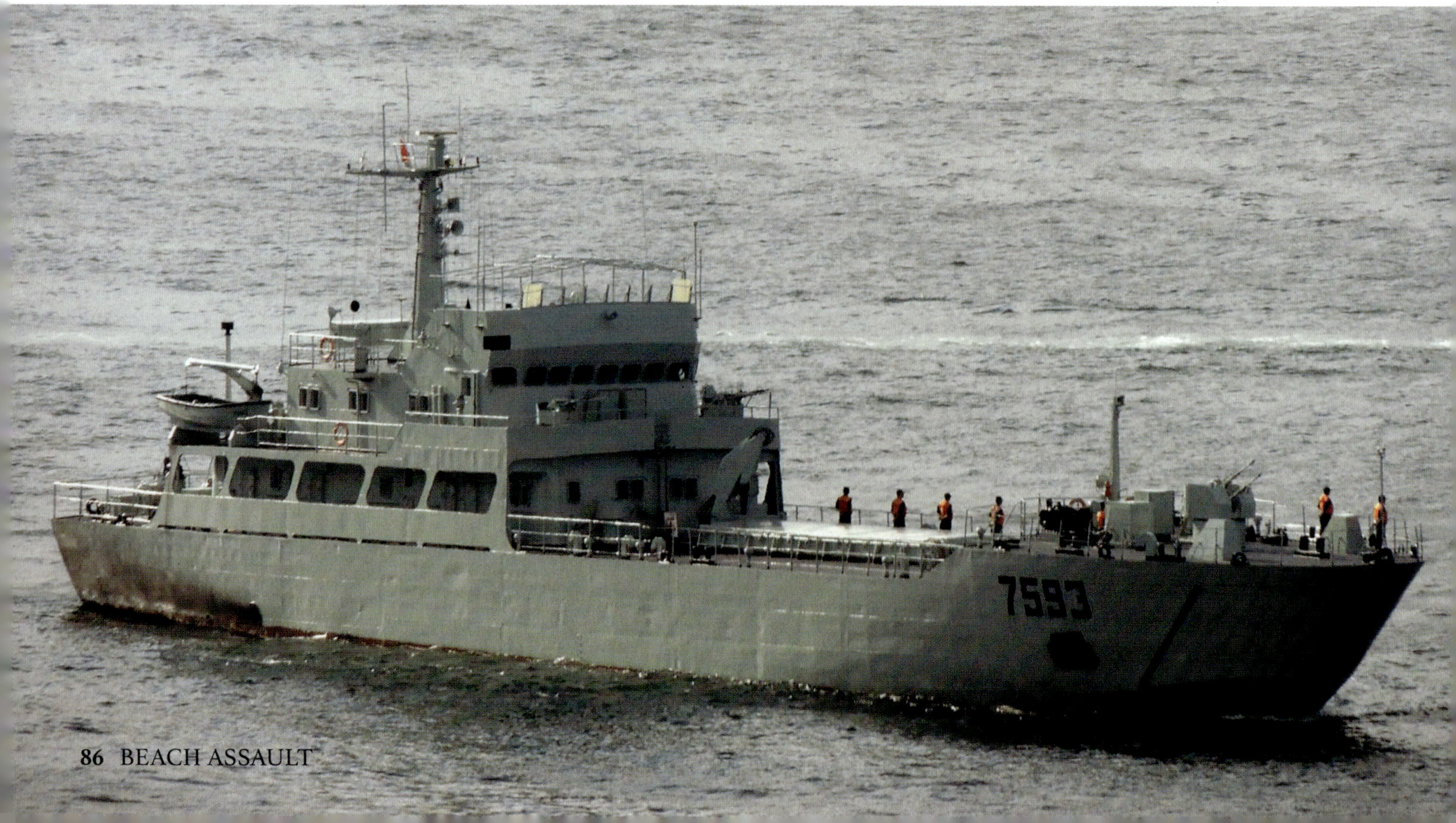

vessels that had limited ocean-going capability.

Since the turn of the century, the PLAN has developed expeditionary ambitions and it started to build ocean going amphibious vessels. When the Indian Ocean was engulfed by piracy emanating from Somalia, from 2008 the Chinese government dispatched navy vessels with marines embarked to join the international maritime security operation. This was the first time a Chinese military contingent had operated outside the country's own territorial waters.

In 2017, the Chinese regularised its presence in the Horn of Africa by establishing a permanent base in Djibouti, including basing amphibious ships and marines there.

The power projection capability of the PLAN amphibious force is centred on its three Type 075-class, landing helicopter dock ships. They have a full-length flight deck for helicopter operations and feature a floodable well deck from which to disembark hovercraft and armoured amphibious assault vehicles. These 40,000-ton ships can each accommodate up to 800 marines and embark 28 helicopters.

The first of class, PLANS *Hainan,* entered service in 2021 and the next two ships were completed by 2022. A fourth ship is under construction.

The next biggest PLAN amphibious ships are the nine Type 071-class amphibious transport dock ships. When they started entering service in 2007, they brought new capabilities that had never been available to the PLAN before.

The Type 071 features a vehicle deck, well-deck, landing deck and a helicopter hangar. It can carry a combination of marines, vehicles, landing craft, and helicopters. The ship can embark 600 to 800 troops. The stern helicopter deck has landing spots for two Z-8 (SA 321 Super Frelon) transport helicopters. The twin-door cantilever hangar can house up to four Z-8 helicopters.

The PLAN operates a mixed fleet of 40 flat bottom landing ships that can load vehicles through bow doors. These vessels have progressively been improved over the past 30 years, with new ships being introduced every couple of years.

A fleet of 40 large hovercraft are operated by the PLAN. It had originally purchased its first Soviet-era military hovercraft from Ukraine and Greece, before beginning to build its own.

The next evolution of the PLAN's amphibious shipping is the Type 076 helicopter carrier, which reportedly is being designed to operate both helicopters and fixed wing combat jets or combat drones. This will mirror the capability of the US Navy's America-class assault ships.

Chile

Armada de Chile

The Chilean navy received a major boost in 2011 when the French built landing ship, FS *Foudre*, was purchased and entered service as the *Sargento Aldea*. She was the lead ship of the Foudre-class, which have all now been retired from the French navy. She has a stern well deck to allow up to eight landing craft to be loaded internally. An embarked force of 450 marines can be carried and four helicopters can also be embarked.

A CDIC-class landing craft utility, the *Soldado Canave*, and two CTM-class landing craft utility, the *Cabo Reyes* and *Soldado Fuentes*,were bought from France to operate from the *Sargento Aldea*.

Chile purchased the plans for the French Champlain-class medium landing ships and built three in its Asmar shipyards in the early 1980s. Two ships, the *Rancagua* and *Chacabuco* remain in service. The flat-bottom ships can ferry over 400 tons of cargo inside their holds or on their upper decks. Loading and unloading can be done from a harbour or on a beach, via a front ramp. Up to 140 marines can be accommodated. A stern landing pad can take light helicopters.

The last of two Orompello-class utility landing craft, the *Elicura,* remains in service. This vessel was built in Chile in 1968. It can accommodate 20 passengers and carry up 350 tons of cargo.

RIGHT: Chilean Navy landing ship *Rancagua* (LST-92) offloading vehicles and troops at Playa San Mateo, Valparaíso. (JOHN CHAPMAN)

BELOW: Chile's main dock landing ship *Sargento Aldea* operates with US Marine Corps CH-46E Sea Knights and a Mexican MI-17 Hind helicopter during Exercise Partnership of the Americas 2014. (US NAVY)

Egypt

Egyptian Naval Force

The Egyptian navy's amphibious capability received a major boost in 2016 when it received two French-built Mistral-class assault ships. These vessels had originally been ordered by Russia, but after Moscow sent its troops to seize Crimea in 2014, France and other European countries imposed an arms embargo.

The French government and the state-owned shipbuilders, DCNS, organised a campaign to find a new buyer for the ships. In August 2015, a €950m deal was concluded with Egypt to buy the vessels and provide long-term training and support.

The 21,000-ton vessels are the largest warships ever operated by the Egyptian navy, so the French offer of support was very important to prepare their new owners to operate them effectively.

Although based on the Mistral-class design used by the French navy, the Russian ships had been modified to meet Moscow's unique requirements, including embarking Ka-52K Alligator attack helicopters. Egypt has a long tradition of operating Soviet and Russian-made equipment, so it quickly started negotiations to buy the Russian attack helicopters and in 2017 signed a contract to buy 46 Ka-52K, which are optimised to operate in the maritime environment.

ENS *Gamal Adbel Nasser* joined exercises with the US Navy in August 2022 in the Mediterranean Sea to rehearse maritime security operations. (US NAVY)

The two ships were in an advanced stage of construction at Saint Nazaire when the Russian order was cancelled. They had even been named. After they were sold to Egypt the ships were renamed. The RFS *Vladivostok* became the ENS *Gamal Abdel Nasser* and RFS *Sevastopol* became the ENS *Anwar El Sadat*. The *Gamal Abdel Nasser* was commissioned in June 2016 and her sister ship entered service three months later.

Since entering service, the two ships have taken part in several amphibious exercises and in September 2023 the ENS *Gamal Abdel Nasser* delivered humanitarian aid to survivors of floods in Libya

BELOW: Egyptian amphibious forces have regularly trained with their US counterparts during the Bright Star series of exercises. (US DOD)

France

Marine Nationale

service in February 2006 and the two sister ships, FS *Tonnerre* and FS *Dixmude*, entered service in December 2006 and December 2012, respectively.

Under French doctrine, they are dubbed 'projection and command ships'. They can embark 16 NH90 or Tiger helicopters, four landing craft, up to 70 vehicles including 13 Leclerc main battle tanks and 450 soldiers. The ships are equipped with a 69-bed hospital and are capable of serving as part of a NATO Response Force, or with United Nations and European Union peace-keeping forces.

The well deck can accommodate four landing craft. The ships are capable of operating two hovercraft to allow them to be interoperate with the United States Marine Corps.

In 2011, the French Army Aviation Tiger and Gazelle armed helicopters embarked on FS *Tonnerre* to launch strike missions against land targets during the Libyan Civil War, as part of joint task force with the British helicopter carrier HMS *Ocean*. In August 2022, the ship was sent to Beirut to deliver humanitarian aid after a huge explosion devastated the Lebanese capital.

ABOVE: The Mistral-class amphibious assault ships have a large stern gate to allow landing craft to enter their well deck. (DAVID MONNIAUX)

BELOW: US Marines embarking aboard the **FNS** *Tonnerre* at Djibouti in December 2017 prior to Franco-US amphibious exercises in the Indian Ocean. (US DOD)

Over the past 25 years the French navy has completely overhauled its amphibious shipping, retiring its helicopter carrier FS *Jeanne d'Arc*, Foudre- and Ouragan-class landing ship dock and Champlai-class landing ship tank.

These have since been replaced by three 21,000-ton Mistral-class 'flattop' amphibious assault ships. The first of class, FS *Mistral*, entered

MISTRAL-CLASS · AMPHIBIOUS ASSAULT SHIP

Displacement: 21,500 tonnes (full load)

Length: 199m (652ft 11in)

Beam: 32m (105ft)

Draught: 6.3m (20ft 8in)

Propulsion: Two x Rolls-Royce Mermaid azimuth thrusters

Speed: 18.8kts (35kph; 22mph)

Range: 5,800nm (10,800km)

Capacity: 70 vehicles, 450 troops

Crew: 160

Armament: Two × Simbad missile systems, 2 x 20mm modèle F2 gun, 2 × 30mm Breda-Mauser, 2 x 7.62mm M134 mini guns

Aircraft carried: 16 heavy or 35 light helicopters

Aviation facilities: Six helicopter landing spots

Italy

Marina Militare

Italy has maintained a strong amphibious shipping force over the past 35 years to embark troops of the San Marco Marine Brigade. The three San Giorgio-class amphibious transport dock ship are multi-role vessels with a 'flattop' helicopter deck. They have a stern well deck to accommodate and load landing craft.

The first two ships, the ITS *San Giorgio* and ITS *San Marco* were commissioned in 1988, and the final ship, the ITS *San Giusto* entered service six years later. They were all built by Fincantieri for the Italian Navy. A modified version has been sold to Algeria and one is on order for Qatar. These 8,000-ton ships can carry a battalion of up to 350 troops, and up to 36 armoured vehicles. The floodable stern dock can accommodate three landing craft.

The first two Italian ships have been modified with longer flight decks with additional helicopter landing spots. ITS *San Giusto*, the third vessel, has not been modified since construction and is normally employed as a training ship.

After more than three decades of service, 21,000-ton replacement ships are starting to be built. They feature a 190m-long flight deck and will be able to accommodate up to 1,000 marines. The first of this new class, the ITS *Trieste*, was launched in 2019 and is nearing completion, with entry to service expected in 2024.

SAN GIORGIO-CLASS AMPHIBIOUS TRANSPORT DOCK

Displacement: 7,960t (7,830 long tons)

Length: 133m (436ft)

Beam: 20.5m (67ft)

Draught: 5.3m (17ft)

Propulsion: Two × Grandi Motori Trieste diesel engines

Speed: 21kts (39kph; 24mph)

Range: 8,000nm (13,900km)

Capacity: 350 troops, 36 tracked armoured vehicles

Crew: 180

Armament: One × Otobreda 76mm gun (removed from San Giorgio and San Marco to increase flight deck space), - two × OTO Melara - Oerlikon KBA 25/80 mm guns

Aircraft carried: Three × AW-101 , five × Agusta Bell AB-212 helicopters or 18 SH90A

Aviation facilities: Flight deck

ABOVE: The three San Giorgio-class assault ships have been central to Italian amphibious operations for three decades. (JACOPO WERTHER)

BELOW: The amphibious transport dock ship ITS *San Marco* underway in the Mediterranean Sea in June 2016 during a NATO Exercise. (US DOD)

Japan

Japanese Maritime Self Defense Force

ABOVE: The Ōsumi class landing ship JS *Shimokita* with a LCAC alongside during a joint UK/Japanese exercise with the Royal Navy amphibious ship, HMS *Albion*. (MOD/CROWN COPYRIGHT)

Japan has a long tradition of building amphibious ships, stretching back to the 1930s when the Imperial Japanese Army commissioned the *Shinshū Maru*, the world's first landing craft carrier ship. She could carry up to 54 landing craft and four armoured gunboats, which could be launched from a floodable well deck.

Over the past 25 years, the modern Japanese Maritime Self Defense Force (JMSDF) has been steadily building up its amphibious capability,

BELOW: Inside the helicopter hangar of JS *Hyūga*. (TOSHINORI BABA)

as tension has grown in the South China Sea. Tokyo is looking to bolster the defences of its remote islands near to Taiwan that have been claimed by China.

In the 1990s work began on the Ōsumi-class landing ships. These 13,000-ton vessels can carry up to 330 marines, eight helicopters and ten main battle tanks, as well as two landing craft or hovercraft in a floodable stern well deck. Three of the ships were built, with the first of class JS *Ōsumi* entering service in 1998.

The following decade the JMSDF began fielding the bigger Hyūga-class helicopter carriers, or helicopter destroyers as the Japanese dubbed them. These ships are optimised for air assault operations with hangar space for up to 18 rotorcraft below deck and accommodation for nearly 400 marines. The 19,000-ton ships entered service from 2001, with the JS *Hyūga* being commissioned first and JS *Ise* following two years later.

JS *Hyūga* had a prominent role in disaster relief operations after the 2011 tsunami caused devastation across Japan.

Work is now underway to convert the JS *Izumo* and its sister ship, JS *Kaga*, into what the JMSDF terms as 'light aircraft carriers' to allow them to embark a combined air-land amphibious task force.

The 27,000-ton JS *Izumo* was commissioned into JMSDF service in 2015. She was then the largest Japanese warship to be built since the end of World War Two. The ship is named after the province of Izuma, and an Imperial Japanese Navy armoured cruiser also bore the name in 1898. Work began at the IHI Marine United shipyard in Yokohama in 2011, with the carrier projected as costing $1.5bn. The JS *Izumo* and her sister ship were originally designated as a 'multi-purpose operation destroyer'

because the country's constitution prohibits the fielding of offensive weapons by the JMSDF that can project power beyond Japan's territorial waters.

Up to 28 helicopters can be embarked on the ship, along with 400 marines and 50 3.5-ton small trucks, with helicopter spots on the deck to allow simultaneous operations by five helicopters.

In December 2018, the Japanese government changed its policy and decided that it would buy F-35B Lightning jump jets so they could be embarked on the Izumo-class ships. Plans were made to convert JS *Izumo* and JS *Kaga* to carry up to 14 F-35Bs and an order for 40 of the jets is in

the process of being placed. Japanese Ground Self Defense Force V-22 Osprey tiltrotors are also expected to operate from the vessels.

The conversion of both ships involved the strengthening of the flight deck by the application of heat-resistant coating to protect it from the hot exhaust from the F-35B's lift-fan system. A new power-supply system was also installed to enable F-35B operations. and her bow shape is also to be changed. The conversion is scheduled to be complete in 2024. A further modification is planned for 2024 to alter the interior compartments to make aircraft maintenance more efficient. There are currently no plans to install a ski jump.

IZUMO-CLASS

Displacement: 27,000 tons

Length: 813ft 8in (248m)

Beam: 124ft 8in (38m)

Draft: 24ft 7in (7.5m)

Propulsion: Four GE/IHI LM2500IEC gas turbines

Speed: 30kts (35mph; 56kph)

Complement: 970 including crew and embarked troops

Armament: Three Phalanx CIWS and two SeaRAM CIWS

Aircraft carried: 28 aircraft or helicopters

ABOVE: The JS *Kaga* is being converted to operate F-35B jump jets to augment her helicopters. (HUNINI)

BELOW: The helicopter carrier JS *Hyuga* during a joint US-Japanese exercise to test amphibious interoperability. (US DOD)

Russia

Russian Federation Navy

ABOVE: The Polish-built Ropucha-class are still the most numerous amphibious landing ship in the Russian navy. (RUSSIAN MINISTRY OF DEFENCE)

BELOW: BTR amphibious armoured personnel carriers 'swim' ashore from the Project 775 or Ropucha-class amphibious landing ship RFS *George Pobedonosets.* (US DOD)

A key enabling capability for Russia's naval infantry and coastal forces are the amphibious vessels assigned to the landing ship brigades.

The Russian Navy currently has a combined total of three Soviet-era Project 1171-class, 14 Project 775-class and two new Iven Gren-class landing ships. The Project 1171- and 775-class vessels are now showing their age and plagued by reliability issues.

Russian amphibious ships have a variety of roles in addition to the delivery of naval infantry units during beach landings in time of war. A major mission since 2015 has been sustaining the Russian garrison in Syria by carrying cargo to it. Amphibious shipping also plays a key role in sustaining isolated Russian outposts in the Arctic and along the country's northern coast where there are no road or rail links to enable land-based logistic support. Russian amphibious ships have played an important role supplying bases on Crimea, since the start of the war with Ukraine in February 2022. Two ships have been lost to Ukrainian missile fire in the war and one badly damaged.

Each of the four Russian fleets - Northern, Baltic, Black Sea, and Pacific - has tailored its amphibious shipping to suit the specific strategic and operational needs and unique geography of its area of operations. Six landings ships from the Northern and Baltic Fleet were redeployed to the Black Sea in February 2022 ahead of the Ukraine war.

The most numerous Russian amphibious landing ship is the Project 775, which is known to NATO as the

Ropucha-class. They were built in Poland for the Soviet Navy at Stocznia Północna shipyards in Gdańsk. They were designed for beach landings and can carry a 450-ton cargo. The ships have both bow- and stern-doors for loading and unloading vehicles, and the 630 square metres of vehicle deck stretches the length of the hull. Up to 25 armoured personnel carriers can be embarked.

While designed for roll-on/roll-off operations, they can also be loaded using dockside cranes. For this purpose, there is a long sliding hatch-cover above the bow section for access to the vehicle deck. There are no facilities for helicopters.

In total, 28 ships of this type were commissioned from 1975 to 1991. The last three ships were of the improved variant Project 775M. These have improved defensive armament and accommodation for a greater number of troops.

Most of the ships became part of the Russian Navy after the dissolution of the Soviet Union and 15 were in service at the start of the war with Ukraine in 2022. In September 2023, the RFS *Minsk* was under repair in the Sevastopol Shipyard when she was hit by a Ukrainian missile attack and damaged beyond repair. In early August 2023, RFS *Olenegorsky Gornyak* was damaged at the Novorossiysk naval base after it was struck by a Ukrainian maritime drone but is now under repair.

The Ivan Gren or Project 11711-class is the newest type of landing ship in Russian service. The 6,600-ton class comprises two vessels, RFS *Ivan Gren* and RFS *Pyotr Morgunov*. The Northern Fleet's 121st Brigade of Landing Ships operates these ships, which were commissioned in June 2018 and December 2020, respectively. Two further ships are being built for the Pacific Fleet.

The vessels of the class have a displacement of 5,000-6,000 tons

and are able to carry up to 13 main battle tanks or 36 armoured personnel carriers and 300 naval infantry.

Attempts to modernise Moscow's amphibious shipping suffered a major setback in 2014 when Western sanctions introduced as a result of the Crimean invasion caused France to cancel the export of two Mistral-class amphibious landing ships to Russia.

In July 2020, the Russian Navy laid down two Project 23900 Universal Landing Ship-class vessels. The ships are estimated to displace 30,000 to 40,000 tons and are intended to carry around 900 naval infantry, ➔

ABOVE LEFT: The Ivan Gren-class are the newest amphibious landing vessels in the Russian navy. (US DOD)

ABOVE RIGHT: The well deck of the RFS *Ivan Gren* can accommodate up to 50 BTR armoured vehicles. (RUSSIAN MINISTRY OF DEFENCE)

RUSSIAN LANDING SHIPS, 2023

Name	Hull Number	Commissioned	Fleet
Project 775			
Olenegorsky Gornyak	12	30-Jun-76	Black Sea
Kondopoga	27	30-Nov-76	Black Sea
Alexandr Otrakovsky	31	30-Jul-78	Black Sea
Project 775/II			
Oslyabya	66	19-Dec-81	Pacific
Admiral Nevelskoy	55	28-Sep-82	Pacific
Kaliningrad	102	09-Dec-84	Baltic
Georgiy Pobedonosets	16	05-Mar-85	Black Sea
Konstantin Olshansky (ex Ukrainian)	154	1985	Black Sea
Alexandr Shabalin	110	31-Dec-85	Baltic
Caesar Kunikov	158	30-Sep-86	Black Sea
Novocherkassk	142	30-Nov-87	Black Sea
Yamal	156	30-Apr-88	Black Sea
Project 775M			
Azov	151	12-Oct-90	Black Sea
Peresvet	77	10-Apr-91	Pacific
Korolev	130	10-Jul-91	Black Sea
Ivan Gren-Class			
Ivan Gren	135	18-May-12	Northern
Pyotr Morgunov	117	25-May-18	Black Sea
Vladimir Andreyev		2023-2025	Pacific
Vasily Trushin		2023-2025	Pacific
Tapir/Alligator-Class			
Orsk	148	31-Dec-68	Black Sea
Nikolay Vilkov	81	30-Jul-74	Pacific
Nikolay Filchenkov	152	30-Dec-75	Black Sea

PROJECT 775/M (ROPUCHA II/M)-CLASS LANDING SHIP

Displacement: 4,080 tons full load

Length: 112.5m (369ft 1in)

Beam: 15m (49ft 3in)

Draft: 3.7m (12ft 2in)

Propulsion: Two × 9,600hp (7,200kW) Zgoda-Sulzer diesel engines

Speed: 18kts (33kph; 21mph)

Range: 6,100nm (11,300km; 7,000 miles)

Endurance: 30 days

Capacity: 10 main battle tanks and 340 troops

Complement: 87–98

Armament: Two × 57mm AK-725 double guns (Ropucha I), one × 76mm AK-176 (Ropucha II), two × 30 122 mm rocket launcher A-215 Grad-M, Strela 2 (SA-N-5) surface-to-air missile system (four launchers), two × 30mm AK-630 six-barrelled Gatling guns (Ropucha II)

75 armoured vehicles and up 20 helicopters. Currently, they are largest warships being built for the Russian Navy. The ships are being constructed but the shipyard at Kerch was hit by a Ukrainian missile strike in 2023, so the status of the project is unclear.

The Project 1171, or Tapir-class, which have the NATO reporting name Alligator, are beach-able landing ships. They have displacement of 4,360 tons when fully loaded and can transport up to 313 troops and 20 tanks. Additional vehicles could be stored on the upper deck. In March 2022, the RFS *Saratov* was sunk by a missile strike while unloading cargo in the captured Ukrainian port of Berdiansk.

RIGHT: The Caspian Sea Flotilla operates several landing craft to support its operations in coastal waters. (ALEX OMEN)

RIGHT: Three Project 1171 or Alligator-class landing ships remain in service. One was lost in a Ukrainian missile strike. (RUSSIAN BLACK SEA FLEET)

South Korea

The ROKN has been steadily building up its amphibious assault capability over the past 30 years with the introduction of new helicopter carriers and landing ships.

The pride of the South Korean navy's amphibious fleet are its two Dokdo-class amphibious assault ship. The 19,500-ton ships were designed and built by Hanjin Heavy Industries (HHIC) and are configured for amphibious assault and humanitarian operations. A third ship is being constructed.

The ships have a well deck to accommodate amphibious assault vehicles (AAVs), landing craft and hovercraft, as well as a full-length flight deck for 10 helicopters. They have accommodation for 720 marines and more than 30 vehicles.

The second ship of the class, ROKS *Marado*, was built with some changes compared to ROKS *Dokdo*, including extra space on the flight deck to accommodate two V-22 Osprey tilt rotors, instead of one on the first of class.

A project was launched in the early 1990s to replace South Korea's World War Two era tank landing ships

(LSTs) with home grown vessels. Four Kojoonbong-class LSTs were built between 1991 and 1998. They can carry up to 12 main battle tanks, which are loaded and unloaded via bow doors.

A second batch of four LSTs, known as the Cheon Wang Bong-class, were delivered between 2014 and 2018. They have a stern well deck to allow two landing craft to be carried internally.

ABOVE: The ROKS *Seongin Bong* tank landing ship en route to the Gulf of Thailand for an exercise with the amphibious dock landing ship USS *Harpers Ferry*. (US NAVY)

BELOW: The ROKS *Dokdo* amphibious dock ship prepares to receive a US Navy LCAC during a joint amphibious exercise. (US NAVY)

Spain

Armada Española

ABOVE: The amphibious assault ship *ESPS* Galicia can launch landing craft and operate helicopters. (STOJAKOVIC81)

Spain's flagship was laid down in 2005 and it was completed five years later to allow the Spanish navy's old aircraft carrier, the *SPS Príncipe de Asturias,* to be retired. The ship is named ESPS *Juan Carlos I*, after the former king.

The ESPS *Juan Carlos I* was initially known as a Strategic Projection Vessel because of its multi-role capabilities. Her crew of 900 can be complemented by another 1,200 marines or passengers.

She has a ski jump to improve the performance of the Spanish navy's AV-8B Harriers. Her flight deck and hangar can accommodate up to 30 helicopters when she is configured for amphibious assault operations or a combination of 12 Harriers and 12 helicopters when operating as an aircraft carrier. The ship's well dock can accommodate four landing craft or a single hovercraft.

BELOW: The amphibious assault ship *Juan Carlos I* is the flag ship of the Spanish navy. (JAVICASELLI)

ESPS *Juan Carlos I* was one of the first major warships to be fitted with diesel-electric propulsion to replace old propeller shafts and it also has a pair of azimuthal pods. These rotate and mean it does not need rudders to direct the ship.

Spain's Navantia shipyards have since sold the design of the vessel to both Australia and Turkey.

The two Galicia -class landing dock ships, both feature large helicopter flight decks and 885sqm well decks for large landing craft, as well as a 1,000sqm space for up to 33 main battle tanks.The Spanish ships were built in co-operation with the Netherlands and the design was also used as the basis for the UK Bay-class.

ESPS *Galicia* was commissioned in 1998 and *ESPS Castilla* in 2000. All three amphibious ships are based at Rota naval base in Spain.

JUAN CARLOS I-CLASS – AMPHIBIOUS ASSAULT SHIP

Displacement: 26,000 long tonnes

Length: 757.3ft (230.82m)

Beam: 105ft (32m)

Draught: 23ft (6.9m)

Propulsion: Two × Propulsion pods

Speed: 21kts (39kph; 24mph)

Compliment: 261 crew, 913 marines and 172 air wing personnel

Armament: Four 20mm guns, Vertical Launch Missile System

Aircraft carried: Up to 25 aircraft and helicopters

Taiwan

Republic of China Navy (ROCN)

The ROCN long relied on the United States to supply its amphibious shipping. This century the nation decided to build its own amphibious ships.

In 2023, the navy took delivery of the first Yushan-class landing platform dock, ROCS *Yushan*. This 10,600-ton multi-role dock landing ship can carry nearly 700 marines and dozens of vehicles, as well as embarking two helicopters. This ship was built by the CSBC Corporation in Taiwan, and it is expected that three more of the vessels will eventually be purchased.

The ROCS *Yushan* incorporates features to reduce its radar signature to prevent adversaries monitoring its movements. It is intended to carry out a full spectrum of amphibious operations, humanitarian relief missions and delivering supplies to remote Taiwanese islands without functioning port facilities.

The next most capable ship in Taiwan's amphibious flotilla is the former USS *Pensacola*, an Anchorage-class dock landing ship. She was transferred to the ROCN in 1999 and renamed the ROCS *Hsu Hai*.

An important role of the ROCN is to move vehicles and cargo to isolated islands close to the coast of mainland China. It retains six tank landing ships for this role, including four ex-US Navy World War Two-era LST-453-class and two ex-US Navy Newport-class vessels. These latter two ships were transferred in 1997 and 2000.

ABOVE: The ROCS *Yushan* was purposed designed for Taiwan's navy to support amphibious operations. (WANG YU CHING/ OFFICE OF THE PRESIDENT)

LEFT: ROCS *Chung Chien* (LST-205) landed US Marines on Okinawa in 1945 before being transferred to the Republic of China Navy in 1948. She still serves 75 years later. (ROC NAVY)

Thailand

Royal Thai Navy (RTN)

The RTN has a long tradition of amphibious warfare and has been investing in new shipping to embark Royal Thai Marine Corps landing units. The 2004 Indian Ocean tsunami hit Thailand hard, and the country's government wanted to invest in new amphibious shipping to increase its ability to deliver humanitarian aid after natural disasters. In April 2023, the RTN took delivery of a Type 071-class landing dock ship, HTMS *Chang (III),* from China's Hudong–Zhonghua Shipbuilding enterprise. This 25,000-ton vessel can embark 800 marines and up to 60 vehicles, as well as four large transport helicopters. Up to four landing craft or hovercraft can be accommodated in the ship's stern well deck.

A Singapore-built Endurance-class landing dock ship, HTMS *Angthong*, was ordered in 2008 and it was delivered four years later. The HTMS *Angthong* was deployed as a base of operations for the navy's humanitarian assistance mission during the 2015 Rohingya refugee crisis, and to provide disaster relief during flooding in southern Thailand in January 2017.

The arrival of the HTMS *Chang (III)* and HTMS *Angthong*, means it is likely that the RTN will be able to retire the aircraft carrier, HTMS *Chakri Naruebet,* which has served as its main amphibious platform up to now.

Additional amphibious lift is provided by two Normed PS 700-class tank landing ships, which were built in Thailand to a French design in the 1980s. The HTMS *Sichang* and HTMS *Surin* are now more than 35 years old and are likely to be the next amphibious ships to be replaced.

RIGHT: The 1980s-era Normed PS 700-class tank landing ship HTMS *Surin* is expected to be retired in the near future. (US DOD)

BELOW: Thailand's navy received the Chinese-built HTMS *Angthong* in April 2023 as part of its drive to build up its amphibious forces. (KEES TORN)

Turkey

Turkish Naval Forces

LEFT: Turkey's amphibious assault ship, TCG *Anadolu*, entered service in April 2023. (TURKISH NAVY)

Turkey has major ambitions for its amphibious forces and has been investing heavily in new shipping. The new pride of the Turkish navy is the TCG *Anadolu*, which was commissioned into the fleet in April 2023. She is a derivative of the Spanish Juan Carlos I-class light aircraft carrier/ amphibious warfare ship.

Construction began at Sedef Shipbuilding Inc. in Istanbul in 2016 with a Turkish-Spanish consortium overseeing the project. Turkish-supplied electronics and other major systems are installed on the ship.

The vessel is intended to undertake long-endurance, long-distance military combat or humanitarian relief operations, while acting as a command centre and flagship for the Turkish Navy.

The arrival of the TCG *Anadolu* expanded dramatically Turkey's amphibious capability, which up to this year did not have a dedicated platform to operate helicopters. Up to 20 helicopters can operate from the new ship and the Turkish navy has ambitions to fly strike drones off her to support of amphibious operations.

The Turkish navy boast six tank landing ships that can unload vehicles and cargo from bow ramps. These include one Osmangazi-class, two Bayraktar-class, two Bey-class landing ship tank and a former US Navy vessel used for training that could be pressed into service in emergencies.

A fleet of more than 30 landing craft are available to support Turkish amphibious operations.

BELOW: The landing ship TCG *Bayraktar* on a visit to Valletta Harbour in Malta. (LSMASTER)

United Kingdom

Royal Navy

The Royal Marines can draw upon a fleet of six amphibious and aviation support ships operated by the Royal Navy and Royal Fleet Auxiliary (RFA). These are highly flexible platforms and when not being used in their traditional amphibious role, they are used to support mine counter-measures and humanitarian missions.

The Royal Navy got its first purpose-built landing ship docks, or LSDs, in the early 1960s when HMS *Fearless* and HMS *Intrepid* entered service. They successfully launched their landing craft into action in San Carlos Water in 1982 during the Falklands war.

In the 1990s, a project to replace the two ships was launched and this culminated in 1996 with an order being placed with the then Vickers Shipbuilding and Engineering Limited, now BAE Systems, in Barrow-in-Furness, to build two new Albion-class LSDs. The ships were designed to function as the afloat command platform for amphibious task force and landing force command staff when embarked, as well as to embark, transport, deploy and recover amphibious troops along with their equipment and vehicles.

As well as a large helicopter deck and purpose-designed command and control facilities, the ships have a large well dock that can hold four Landing Craft Utility (LCU) Mark 10s and four smaller Landing Craft Vehicle Personnel (LCVP) Mark

ALBION-CLASS - LANDING PLATFORM DOCK

Displacement: 19,560 tons

Length: 176m (577ft)

Beam: 28.9m (95ft)

Draught: 7.1m (23ft)

Propulsion: GE Power Conversion Full Electric

Speed: 18kts (21mph; 33kph)

Range: 13,000km (7,000nm)

Crew: 325

Capacity: 67 vehicles, 405 Royal Marines (710 surge)

Armament: Two × 20mm Phalanx CIWS, two × 20 mm cannon

Aviation facilities: Two landing spots for helicopters up-to the size of a Chinook

5s. There is an internal articulated ramp that leads up to the ship's vehicle deck, which allows the landing craft to be loaded within the sheltered well dock, before exiting from the rear gate. Each ship also carries a 52-ton tracked beach recovery vehicle for assisting with landing craft recovery, as well as two tractors: one that can lay a trackway across a landing beach, and the second fitted with an excavating bucket and forks.

The design of the ships is inherently flexible, allowing assault troops either to be loaded on landing craft or carried ashore by helicopter. In surge mode, more than 400 troops can be carried aboard each ship. However, the ships do not have hanger decks to allow helicopters to be maintained in heavy weather and rough seas.

The 2010 defence cuts considerably reduced the UK's high readiness amphibious forces and to save money it was decided to only keep one of the

LSDs in frontline service at a time. The ships would alternate between what was termed 'extended readiness periods' tied up in Devonport dockyard. This was usually around two years at a time, although the Royal Navy said in time of crisis the tied-up ship could be rapidly brought back into service.

The three Bay-class LSDs were purchased to replace the old Knights of the Round Table-class landing ships that have provided sterling service for nearly 40 years. The images of the

ABOVE: HMS *Bulwark* **led an Anglo-French naval task force in 2014.** (MOD/CROWN COPYRIGHT)

LEFT: The large dock on the Albion-class landing ships provides a home to a variety of landing craft and small boats operated by Royal Marines. (MOD/CROWN COPYRIGHT)

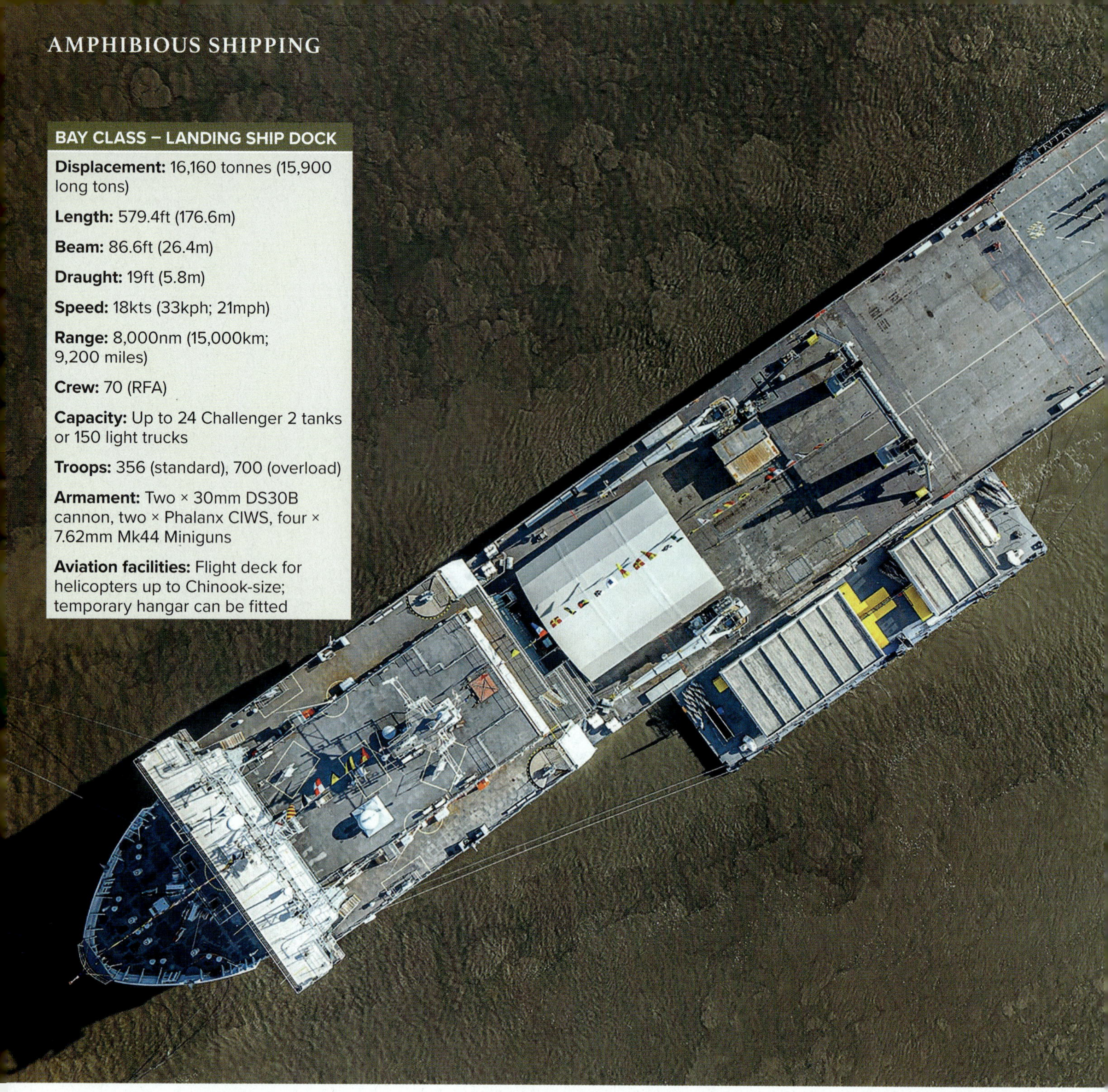

BAY CLASS – LANDING SHIP DOCK

Displacement: 16,160 tonnes (15,900 long tons)

Length: 579.4ft (176.6m)

Beam: 86.6ft (26.4m)

Draught: 19ft (5.8m)

Speed: 18kts (33kph; 21mph)

Range: 8,000nm (15,000km; 9,200 miles)

Crew: 70 (RFA)

Capacity: Up to 24 Challenger 2 tanks or 150 light trucks

Troops: 356 (standard), 700 (overload)

Armament: Two × 30mm DS30B cannon, two × Phalanx CIWS, four × 7.62mm Mk44 Miniguns

Aviation facilities: Flight deck for helicopters up to Chinook-size; temporary hangar can be fitted

ABOVE: RFA *Mounts Bay* **seen from above as the ship's company parade on her flight deck in hour of HM The Queen's Platinum Jubilee.** (MOD/CROWN COPYRIGHT)

RIGHT: RFA *Mounts Bay* **in a Norwegian fjord after landing Royal Marines ashore for an Arctic warfare exercise.** (MOD/CROWN COPYRIGHT)

RFA *Sir Galahad* on fire at Bluff Cove in the Falklands war in 1982 made the landing ships iconic. They were considered an essential component of the Royal Navy amphibious shipping flotilla that supported the Royal Marines. When not participating in amphibious exercises or operations the landing ships moved dangerous stores, such as artillery ammunition and missiles, between the UK and overseas British Army garrisons.

The new ships were based on the existing Dutch-Spanish Royal Schelde Enforcer-class, with some modifications to be the basis of the new Bay class vessels.

They feature a large well dock that can accommodate two landing craft and two Mexeflote ferries. There is

Although owned by the Royal Navy, they are mostly crewed by civilian sailors. In 2010, the new Conservative-led coalition government ordered a round of defence cuts, including reduction in the amphibious shipping fleet. One of the Bay-class LSDs was sold off and ended up in the Royal Australian Navy as the HMAS *Choules*.

In RFA service the remaining three Bay-class vessels have been highly active in many roles, including providing humanitarian relief in the Caribbean, hosting training for the Iraqi navy and providing a mothership capability for Royal Navy mine counter measures vessels in the Arabian Gulf. More recently they have been used as trials vessels to host unmanned craft.

The ships are now playing a key role in the development of the Littoral Strike Groups concept and are playing host to detachments of Royal Marines equipped with raiding craft, attack helicopters and unmanned aerial vehicles. Eventually the Royal Navy proposes to buy purpose built Littoral Strike Ships, but the project has been delayed until after 2030 so the Bay-class will have a role to play in Littoral Strike operations by the Royal Marines until then.

The RFA also operates the aviation support ship RFA *Argus,* which can also be re-roled as a hospital ship, or Primary Casualty Receiving Ship (PCRS) as it is known. In 2014, the ship was dispatched to Sierra Leone to provide medical support to counter the outbreak of the deadly Ebola virus. She has since been re-roled as an interim Littoral Strike Ship and, in the autumn of 2023, deployed to the Mediterranean and Middle East with a Royal Marines company and Fleet Air Arm helicopters embarked. This deployment is trialling the Littoral Response Group concept in hot climates.

an internal ramp to allow the landing craft or ferries to be loaded inside the vessel at sea. The ships also have steerable azimuth thrusters which allow them to be manoeuvred into small harbours or close to shorelines. The rear ramp can be used to load vehicles from quay sides or at commercial ferry terminals. Two 30-ton capacity cranes can lift ISO containers onto the deck without the need for shore-based loading systems.

Unlike the Dutch versions, the British Bay-class do not have an enclosed hanger to support aviation operations. The flight deck can accommodate several helicopters, including sizes up to the big Chinook.

The four ships proved to be highly effective vessels after they entered service from 2006 with the RFA.

United States of America

US Navy

RIGHT: The Wasp-class assault ship, USS *Boxer*, hosted Australian S70A Black Hawk helicopters during a join exercise in the Pacific. (US NAVY)

BELOW: The Whidbey Island-class dock landing ship USS *Tortuga* (LSD 46) was moored pier side in New Orleans to host victims of Hurricane Katrina, providing them with hot meals, showers, and beds to sleep in.
(US NAVY)

Known as the 'gator navy' or 'green water navy', the US Navy's amphibious ships are designed to dominate littoral waters close to the coasts of potential opponents or enemy nations.

The US Navy provides the amphibious shipping that delivers the US Marines to their operational theatres. These ships are developed jointly by the two services to ensure they are optimised for amphibious operations, including the design of aircraft hangers, well decks, troop accommodation and communication arrays.

This symbiotic relationship began before World War Two when the two services began co-operating in the Fleet Marine Force experiment. This led to the development of a whole family of landing ships and landing craft that were used during the Pacific island-hopping campaign, as well as on D-Day. All these vessels had to be designed to be interoperable and interchangeable.

In a modern context, every piece of equipment used by the US Marines needs to be able to fit on US Navy amphibious ships and landing craft. Aircraft and helicopters need to be able to be parked inside assault ship's hanger decks. Landing craft need to

be able to be manoeuvred into well decks. By working closely together at the design stage, the US Navy and US Marines now have a very effective fleet of power projection ships.

The evolution of amphibious ship design is reflected in the US Navy's current fleet. When the US Marine Corps started to introduce large numbers of helicopters in the early 1960s to carry out 'vertical envelopment' during amphibious operations, the US Navy at first converted surplus aircraft carriers to be helicopter carriers. In the 1970s the first purpose designed helicopter carriers appeared.

The next evolution was the arrival of the Landing Craft Air Cushion (LCAC) in the early 1980s which meant the design of dock ships needed to be modified to accommodate them. In the 21st century, the introduction of the MV-22B Osprey tilt rotor offered the potential to carry out long range insertion operations. This led some to suggest that well decks to launch landing craft could be deleted from the new America-class assault ships. However, that was judged to be a premature decision and the well deck was reintroduced in the later ships of the America-class.

The US Navy now operates nine 'flat top' assault ships, which have helicopter decks, and all but two have well decks to accommodate and launch landing craft.

These big assault ships are supported by 22 dock landing ships and these vessels have a key role acting as floating bases for landing craft and hovercraft. Although the importance of helicopters in US Marine Corps assault operations is well known, landing craft are still fundamental to deliver bulk quantities of 'heavy metal' logistics support from ship to shore. Bulk quantities of fuel, water, and ammunition can only really be delivered ashore by large vehicles carried in landing craft. ➤

US NAVY – ASSAULT SHIPS, 2023

Name	Hull number	Launched	Commissioned
Wasp-Class			
USS Wasp	LHD-1	04-Aug-87	29-Jul-89
USS Essex	LHD-2	23-Feb-91	17-Oct-92
USS Kearsarge	LHD-3	26-Mar-92	16-Oct-93
USS Boxer	LHD-4	13-Aug-93	11-Feb-95
USS Bataan	LHD-5	15-Mar-96	20-Sep-97
USS Iwo Jima	LHD-7	04-Feb-00	30-Jun-01
USS Makin Island	LHD-8	22-Sep-06	24-Oct-09
America-Class			
Flight 0			
USS America	LHA-6	04-Jun-12	11-Oct-14
USS Tripoli	LHA-7	01-May-17	15-Jul-20
Flight I			
USS Bougainville	LHA-8	06-Oct-23	In 2024
USS Fallujah	LHA-9		

ABOVE: In July 2020 the USS *Bonhomme Richard* was devastated by fire in San Diego and was so badly damaged, she had to be scrapped. (US NAVY)

BELOW: The US Navy operates amphibious ready groups, combining different types of ships to bring multiple capabilities into play during amphibious operations. (US NAVY)

US Navy amphibious ships are designed to operate either as part of a large amphibious task force or to carry out tasks independently. One assault ship and two dock landing ships are usually grouped together to form an Amphibious Ready Group, or ARG, to carry a battalion-sized marine expeditionary unit.

The America-class of amphibious assault ships are eventually intended to replace the eight Wasp-class vessels. They each cost $2.4bn to build and incorporated many of the features trialled on the USS *Makin*, the last of the Wasp-class, including gas turbines and enhanced electrical systems. The first two ships of the America-class, known as Flight 0 vessels, are intended to use only airlift to deliver their marines to shore so do not have a well deck to accommodate landing craft. This allows extra-space for fuel and other aviation support facilities. Potentially, America-class vessels can accommodate a full load of 20 F-35B Lightning jump jets but are normally intended to operate a marine expeditionary unit that combines F-35Bs or AV-8B Harriers, MV-22B Osprey tilt-rotors, CH-35 Sea Stallion heavy lift helicopters, UH-1Y Huey utility helicopters, and AH-1W Cobra helicopter gunships. The first of the ships was formally commissioned into the US Navy in 2014.

The second of class, USS *Tripoli*, is the third US Navy vessel to be named after the first land battle fought on foreign soil by the US Marines in 1805. The battle is memorialised in the US Marines' hymn with the line, "to the shores of Tripoli". Three more ships of the class are being built.

ABOVE: USS *America* is the lead ship of the America-class, and it is optimised for air insertion operations. (US NAVY)

RIGHT: The amphibious assault ship USS *Tripoli* commissioned in July 2020. The second ship in the America-class was named for the Battle of Derne in 1805, which the US Marine Corps commemorate as the battle honour, Tripoli. (US NAVY)

Work on the USS *Wasp* began in 1985 as part of a major expansion of the US Navy's amphibious capabilities in the final decade of the Cold War. She was finally commissioned in 1989, only a few months before the collapse of the Berlin Wall. The design of the ship, with her large well deck for landing craft and two hangars to support aircraft operations, proved to be ideal for the conflicts and humanitarian crises that unfolded in the 1990s and 2000s. As a result, the US Navy maintained a drum beat of orders for eight Wasp-class vessels through to 2002 when the last ship, USS *Makin Island*, was ordered.

The USS *Wasp* sailed for her maiden operational deployment in 1991 with a marine expeditionary unit embarked. She played an important role in Operation Restore Hope in Somalia in 1993. Over the next decade she was a mainstay of US Atlantic Fleet deployments, including to the Mediterranean and Middle East.

From 2004 the USS *Wasp* was very active supporting US combat operations in Iraq and Afghanistan. In 2007 she carried out the first operational deployment of an MV-22B Osprey squadron. She had previously trialled the Osprey during the early stages of the programme in the 1990s.

During 2011 she was modified to operate the F-35B and the USS *Wasp* then carried out the first sea trials with the new jump jet to prepare to bring the aircraft into service. Two years later the USS *Wasp* was the first US Navy warship to go to sea on an operational cruise with a detachment of F-35Bs embarked. All the Wasp-class ships remain in service, apart

from the USS *Bonhomme Richard*, which was scrapped after being devastated by a dockyard fire in April 2021

The newest type of amphibious dock landing ship in US Navy service is the San Antonio-class. These replace the Austin-class dock ships, including Cleveland and Trenton sub-classes, as well as the Newport-class tank landing ships, the Anchorage-class dock landing ships, and

AMERICA-CLASS

Displacement: 44,971 long tons

Length: 844ft (257m)

Beam: 106ft (32m)

Draft: 26ft (7.9m)

Propulsion: Two gas turbines, two shafts

Speed: Over 22kts (41kph; 25mph)

Complement: 1,049 crew, plus 1,687 embarked Marines with a 184-surge capacity

Armament: Two Rolling Airframe Missile launchers, two Evolved Sea Sparrow Missile launchers, two 20mm Phalanx CIWS, two x 25mm M242 Bushmaster machine gun system

Aircraft carried: 32 fixed wing aircraft or helicopters

LEFT: **MV-22 Ospreys** prepare to launch from the amphibious assault ship USS *Wasp* during a deployment to the Middle East in 2007. (US NAVY)

BELOW: US Navy sailors unload equipment from a landing craft, air cushion (LCAC) in the well deck aboard the amphibious assault ship USS *Wasp*. (US NAVY)

WASP-CLASS

Displacement: 40,500 long tons

Length: 843ft (257m)

Beam: 104ft (31.8m)

Draft: 27ft (8.1m)

Propulsion: Two boilers, two geared steam turbines, two shafts

Speed: 22kts (41kph; 25mph)

Complement: 1,070 crew, with 1,687 embarked marine contingent, as well as 184 surge capacity.

Armament: Two RIM-116 Rolling Airframe Missile launchers, two RIM-7 Sea Sparrow missile launchers, three 20mm Phalanx CIWS systems (LHD 5–8 with two), four 25mm Mk38 chain guns

Aircraft carried: 26 fixed wing aircraft or helicopters

ABOVE: The amphibious transport dock ships USS *San Antonio* and USS *New York* take part in joint manoeuvres in the Atlantic. (US NAVY)

BELOW: The inner workings of the San Antonio –class show that they are complex vessels. (US NAVY)

the Charleston-class amphibious cargo ships. The arrival of the USS *San Antonio* in 2006 allowed the retirement of all these legacy vessels to begin.

The San Antonio-class were the first dock ships to be purpose designed to accommodate LCACs and two can be carried. They were also the first US dock ships to be built with a permanent helicopter hangar.

The 13 ships of the San Antonio-class were originally pitched at costing $890m each but ended up costing nearly double that figure. The early ships of the class were plagued with technical problems that nearly led to the class being cancelled. An order for the 13th ship in the main class was placed in 2018 and is in the process of being fitted out to enter service.

A new variant of the class, known as Flight II, was ordered in 2018 and this is intended to be a replacement for the Whidbey Island-class dock ships. The US Navy had planned to build 13 Flight II ships. One is currently being constructed, two are on contract and funding for the remainder of the ships has been put on hold.

The Whidbey Island-class was introduced into US Navy service in 1985 and it was the first dock ship that was capable of holding four LCAC hovercraft. Five can be carried if the vehicle ramp is raised. The class also had multiple cranes and a shallow draft that further make it ideal for participating in amphibious operations.

All ships of the class underwent a midlife upgrade up to 2014 to ensure that they remain in service through to 2038. Major elements of the upgrade package include diesel engine improvements, fuel and maintenance savings systems, engineering control systems, increased air conditioning and chill water capacity, and replacement of air compressors.

The Harpers Ferry-class of dock landing ships started being delivered in the early 1990s. They were

US NAVY - DOCK LANDING SHIPS, 2023

Ship Name	Hull No.	Launched	Commissioned	Proposed Retirement
Whidbey Island-Class				
USS Germantown	LSD-42	29-Jun-84	08-Feb-86	2023
USS Gunston Hall	LSD-44	27-Jun-87	22-Apr-89	2023
USS Comstock	LSD-45	15-Jan-88	03-Feb-90	2026
USS Tortuga	LSD-46	15-Sep-88	17-Nov-90	2023
USS Rushmore	LSD-47	06-May-89	01-Jun-91	2024
USS Ashland	LSD-48	11-Nov-89	09-May-92	2023
Harpers Ferry-Class				
USS Harpers Ferry	LSD-49	15-Apr-91	07-Jan-95	2024
USS Carter Hall	LSD-50	11-Nov-91	30-Sep-95	2023
USS Oak Hill	LSD-51	21-Sep-92	08-Jun-96	2025
USS Pearl Harbor	LSD-52	27-Jan-95	30-May-98	2024
San Antonio-Class				
Flight I				
USS San Antonio	LPD-17	12-Jul-03	14-Jan-06	
USS New Orleans	LPD-18	11-Dec-04	10-Mar-07	
USS Mesa Verde	LPD-19	19-Nov-04	15-Dec-07	
USS Green Bay	LPD-20	11-Aug-06	24-Jan-09	
USS New York	LPD-21	19-Dec-07	07-Nov-09	
USS San Diego	LPD-22	07-May-10	19-May-12	
USS Anchorage	LPD-23	12-Feb-11	04-May-13	
USS Arlington	LPD-24	23-Nov-10	08-Feb-13	
USS Somerset	LPD-25	14-Apr-12	01-Mar-14	
USS John P. Murtha	LPD-26	30-Oct-14	08-Oct-16	
USS Portland	LPD-27	13-Feb-16	14-Dec-17	
USS Fort Lauderdale	LPD-28	28-Mar-20	30-Jul-22	
USS Richard M. McCool Jr.	LPD-29	05-Jan-22		
Flight II				
USS Harrisburg	LPD-30			
USS Pittsburgh	LPD-31			
USS Philadelphia	LPD-32			

modified from the Whidbey Island-class design, sacrificing landing craft capacity for more cargo space, making it closer to an amphibious transport dock. It has a shorter well deck and can only carry two LCACs.

Externally, the two classes can be distinguished by the positions of weapons. The Harpers Ferry-class has the Phalanx CIWS mounted forward, and the RAM launcher on top of the bridge, while the Whidbey Island-class has the opposite arrangement.

The LX(R)-class, formerly LSD(X)-class, had been proposed as a new class of amphibious dock ship. It is intended to be a replacement for the current Whidbey Island-class and Harpers Ferry-class dock landing ships from 2025 or 2026, and to replace them all by 2039. This programme has since been halted to allow a major review of all US Navy amphibious shipping.

ABOVE: USS *Harpers Ferry* has a flight deck but no hanger to protect embarked helicopters from bad weather. (US NAVY)

BELOW: The amphibious dock landing ship USS *Fort McHenry* supported disaster relief and humanitarian efforts in the wake of the Tsunami that struck southeast Asia. in 2005. (US NAVY)

Beach Assault into the 21st Century

Applying New Tech to Amphibious Operations

ABOVE: Putting troops ashore on enemy-held coasts is still the aim of amphibious operations, but new technology is augmenting age old tactics and techniques. (MOD/CROWN COPYRIGHT)

More than 100 nations have military units that they designate as marines, or specialists in amphibious operations. Dozens of navies operate the specialist amphibious shipping needed to deliver their marines on to enemy held coasts. The nature of warfare has changed dramatically since World War Two and this has transformed how amphibious operations are executed. The Hollywood movie *Saving Private Ryan* has entered public consciousness as what beach assaults were all about in World War Two. Landing craft full of infantrymen storming up a beach in the face of deadly German machine gun fire.

In the 1950s and 1960s, the introduction of the helicopter led to a new era of amphibious warfare, with marines being moved ashore by air and avoiding having to fight the enemy on the beaches. The British experience in Al Faw in 2003 showed that amphibious operations in complex littoral environments needed to incorporate air, land, sea, and surveillance capabilities into a joint force.

In the 21st century, the nature of amphibious warfare is undergoing rapid transformation due to the proliferation of long-range weapons to defend coastlines and the development of unmanned or robotic systems. These trends have made it even more unlikely that the scenes on Utah Beach in Normandy will be repeated by the modern generation of amphibious warriors.

Many nations have looked at how they could prevent the US and its allies carrying out amphibious operations and then worked out that this could best be achieved by fielding long range, precision guided anti-ship and air defence surface to air missiles, backed up by super silent submarines and fourth- and fifth generation fighter jets. This

RIGHT: Ukrainian missile strikes on Russian ports and shipping in the Black Sea region have highlighted the vulnerability of big amphibious ships to attack. (MAXAAR TECHNOLOGIES)

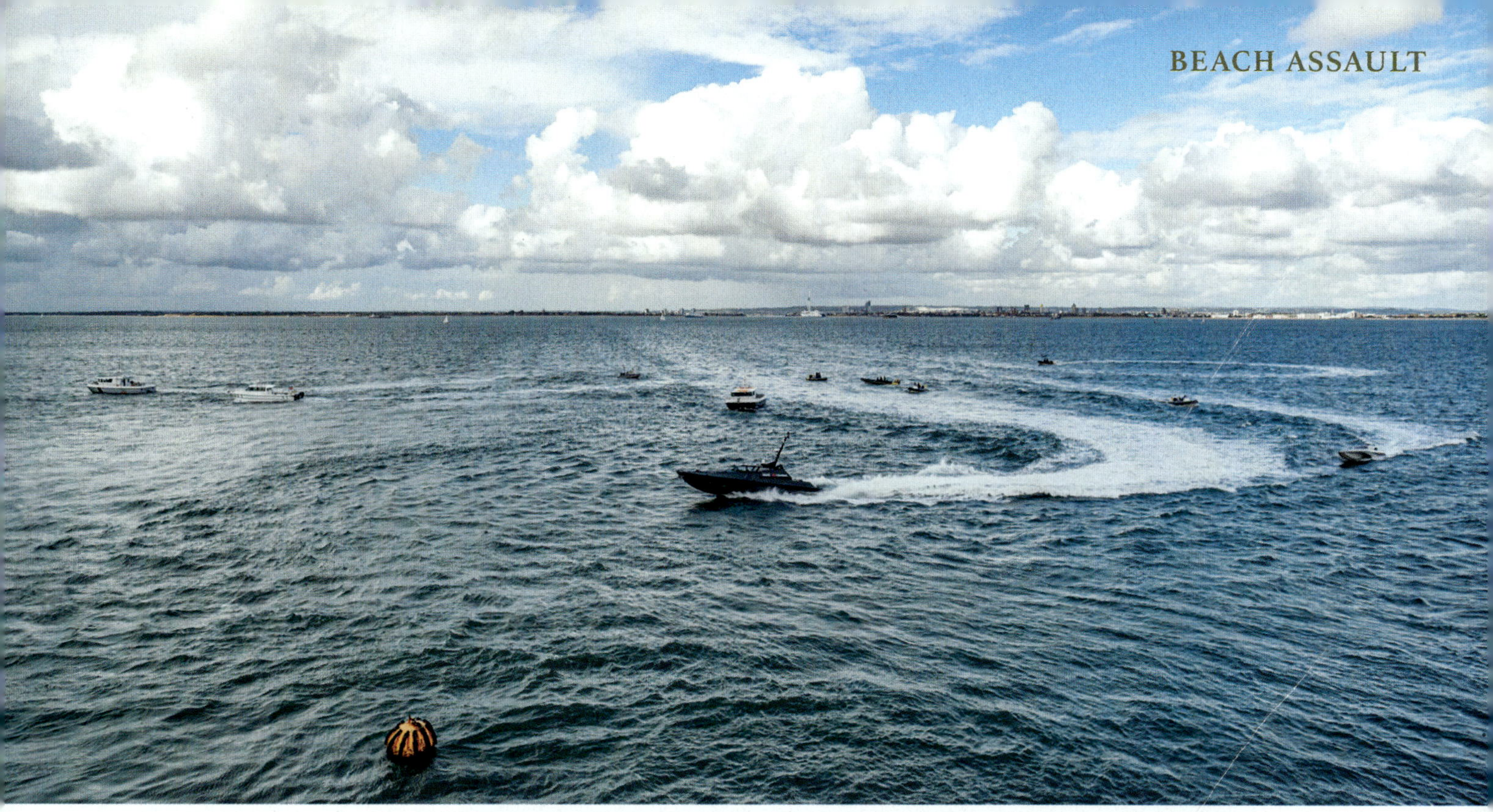

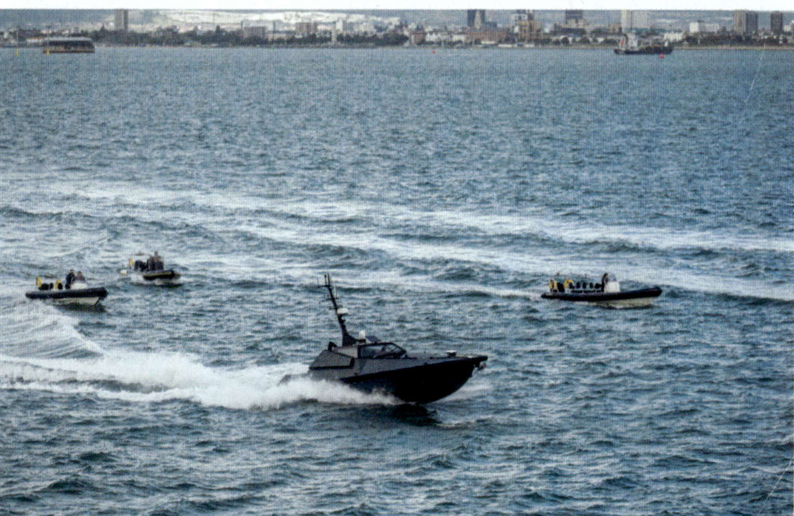

has entered the lexicon of military jargon as Anti-Access, Area Denial, or A2AD, warfare.

China and Russia are the leaders in developing A2AD capabilities, and their declared aim is to dominate the sea zones around their countries to stop the US and its allies projecting power into their 'back gardens'. Russian missile arrays, or umbrellas, in the Black Sea, Baltic Sea, and Arctic regions and Chinese coastal defences in the South China Sea are all now in place. This reality is making western naval commanders very cautious about moving their warships into range of them. Other nations, such as Iran, Algeria, Vietnam, and Ukraine have developed their own version of A2AD to protect their own coastlines.

This has major implications for future amphibious operations. It means large amphibious vessels cannot risk heading close to shore until enemy missile defences have been neutralised. This is not just a case of knocking out anti-ship missile batteries but also long-range air defences because of the risk they pose to vital troop transport helicopters. It also calls into question how viable it is to use big dock ships to launch landing craft, if they can no longer come close to shore to deliver them.

So, what is the answer to this challenge? Some in the US Navy think it has the size, ambition, and budget to contemplate launching theatre level campaigns to destroy all the elements of A2AD defences. Others are not so sure, and believe a more radical solution is needed, both on cost grounds and because they say it will not be possible to knock out every enemy missile battery.

One idea is to move away from large ships and distribute the landing force among many smaller transport ships and new ocean-going landing craft. This is a return to the World War Two era small landing ships that could each carry around a dozen vehicles or a company of 100 marines. In simple terms, this spreads the risk so that a lucky hit against a large assault ship will not take out the bulk of any landing force.

Next, a new generation of assault helicopters are being examined. The US Boeing MV-22B Osprey tilt rotor has shown the potential for long range insertion of amphibious forces. However, they cost $84m each, and high operating costs meant that only the US and Japan operate this unique capability. The Pentagon is already working with US aerospace companies to develop next the generations of tilt rotor craft and if the price can be cut then amphibious force around the world could benefit from them.

Unmanned, or robotic technology, is developing at a rapid pace and several nations are now applying it to amphibious operations. The critical beach reconnaissance phase of amphibious assaults is starting to benefit from this new technology.

Small hand-launched, unmanned aerial vehicles, or drones as they are popularly known, are in widespread use with marine units. They can be launched from small boats or landing craft to overfly beaches to provide real-time intelligence of enemy defences or environmental conditions.

Ukrainian forces have made extensive use of robot or remote-controlled boats to strike at Russian warships and naval bases. Marine commanders around the world are keen to buy similar vessels to carry out covert beach reconnaissance missions or carry explosives to demolish enemy defences.

ABOVE: Swarms of robot boats have been used to devastating effect by the Ukrainians against Russian forces in the Black Sea. (MOD/CROWN COPYRIGHT)

LEFT: Allied navies, including Britain, are conducting extensive experiments with robot boats for a variety of roles, including amphibious operations. (MOD/CROWN COPYRIGHT)

The artificial intelligence (AI) technology being used to make driverless cars safe to operate on roads could be re-purposed for use in driverless landing craft. They in turn could deliver unmanned combat vehicles or supply vehicles to beachheads. The on-line shopping company, Amazon, is already experimenting with using flying drones to deliver shopping to customer's back gardens. US Marines and the Royal Marines are examining this technology to move supplies ashore and also to collect casualties for evacuation.

This all contributes to reducing the size of amphibious landing forces and in turn reducing the amount of shipping needed to carry them. Fewer ships mean less targets for enemy missiles.

Already, many navies are looking to field flotillas of armed robot boats to replace the rigid inflatable craft they use to patrol in coastal waters. These craft have obvious applications in littoral operations, where amphibious forces need to dominate coastal waters to protect their shipping from attack during landing operations.

These developments all have the potential to revolutionise amphibious warfare, but many observers say they will not remove the need for highly specialised personnel to plan and execute amphibious operations.

It takes years to build up understanding of the unique maritime environment in coastal regions and then regular training is needed to drill amphibious personnel in how to cope with the unexpected events that always occur when marines come ashore on hostile coastlines.

No matter how much automation, robotics, and smart AI technology is brought to bear, the central lessons of more than a century of amphibious warfare still applies today. Amphibious warriors operate in extreme environments, where tides, storms, and shifting sands can all conspire to throw a spanner in the works, at a moment's notice. It takes experienced and adaptable sailors and marines to react to whatever Mother Nature throws at them. This is the human element of amphibious warfare that will probably never be able to be replicated and replaced by robots.